LIVING OVER THE SHOP

COOKING FROM THE TOP LEVEL

BY STEVEN DOHERTY

Foreword by Albert Roux

FOREWORD BY ALBERT ROUX
CBE, LEGION D'HONNEUR

It is a great pity that I do not have enough words to express my admiration for Steven.

He first appeared in my life as a young commis chef straight from The Savoy and faithfully stayed with me at the stove for a number of years where I had first view of his dedication and hard work on a daily basis.

I had no hesitation to arrange for him to work in France with a dear departed friend of mine, Alain Chapel, where he worked for two years and came back to me as a chef de cuisine at Le Gavroche. He certainly did play a big part in Le Gavroche being the first restaurant in the UK to be awarded three Michelin stars.

He went on to enjoy further success in his next challenge. It certainly showed what type of a man Steven is. There was no need for him to have caviar and foie gras to cook to perfection and the pub he was managing won great acclaim.

I am sure that you will read his book with great interest and make good use of it.

CONTENTS

INTRODUCTION

I'm often asked what is the secret behind Lakeland's success. The answer is perfectly straightforward. Ever since we started out in the 1960s we've insisted the customer receives two things – the highest quality, paired with value for money.

It's a formula we applied when we decided to open a café above our flagship store in Windermere. It was essential the menu reflected the same quality and high standards as the kitchenware we had become famous for.

That menu had to provide variety, originality, locally sourced ingredients, top quality service and value. There could scarcely have been anyone in the country better qualified to take on the challenge than Steven Doherty. His Roux brothers training, vast Michelin-starred know-how, local foodie knowledge and extensive gastro pub experience convinced us that he and Marj were the right people to run the café.

Beginning as an 18-year old apprentice at The Savoy back in 1976, Steven spent many successful years learning and then mastering his trade within London and further afield in Europe. On relocating to the Lake District in the 1990s, Steven and Marj took the helm first at the Brown Horse at Winster and then The Punch Bowl at Crosthwaite, gaining much praise locally and receiving a number of highly acclaimed awards, as well as a raft of highly-contented diners.

We had no doubt that Steven would bring his unique blend of skill and knowledge to the café, and indeed it's testimony to his success that lunchtimes are full most days of the week. Customers are more than happy to wait and, of course, they can do a little shopping until their table becomes available.

Steven shares the same values and beliefs about kitchenware and creative cooking with everybody at Lakeland – a love of wholesome, home-made food made simple, the freshest ingredient cooked and presented to perfection. This has proved to be a winning partnership to the extent that a trip to our flagship store just wouldn't be complete without a visit to the café. With Steven's guidance, we've taken a creative, contemporary approach, and our modern, welcoming venue offers restaurant-quality dishes in a relaxed atmosphere with panoramic views across to the Lakeland Fells (weather permitting!).

It was with great delight that myself and my brothers Martin and Julian first seized the opportunity to work with Steven back in 2003, and in the same way it's an absolute honour for us to write the introduction to this book. Everyone at Lakeland has tremendous respect for what Steven and Marj have achieved in what has proved so far to be an illustrious career, and we look forward to the continuing success of what has proved to be a perfect partnership.

Sam Rayner

ACKNOWLEDGEMENTS

We owe a huge debt of gratitude to the following bodies
that made this book possible, they are:-

Albert Henri Roux for everything you taught me and so much more...

Marj's Mum and Dad who helped us financially at the beginning
of the journey in Crosthwaite

Allan Bell and Lionel Yates, our former business partners in
The Punch Bowl, who helped get us started

Sam, Julian and Martin Rayner for giving us the opportunity to work with them,
for the many enjoyable moments at Lakeland and a life!

Allan and Sandra, our most loyal Heads of Departments in the First Floor,
who run the day to day in the Café that have allowed us the time to fulfil
my ambition to write a book

Richard Rose and **Sue and Jem Francis** for allowing their charming kitchens and
gardens to be used in the shots

Valerie and John Harrison for their eyes and ears

Martin Edwards, Paul Cocker, Jodi Hinds and Susan Pape at
The Regional Magazine Company Limited for their patience and professional
expertise in producing such a stunning book, beyond our imagining

Our suppliers, some of whom have been serving us for nearly 20 years

Angelo and Clare Cutolo, cherished friends of the Villa Positano,
the first restaurant we visited when we moved up to the Lakes
– your generosity and kindness knows no bounds

Steven & Marj Doherty

Written by:
Steven & Marj Doherty
First Floor Café
Alexandra Buildings
Windermere
LA23 1BQ
(015394) 88100

Edited by:
Martin Edwards, Chris Brierley
RMC Books – (0114) 250 6300

Design by:
Paul Cocker, David Pass
RMC Books – (0114) 250 6300

Photography by:
Jodi Hinds – www.jodihinds.com

Contributors:
Susan Pape, Nicola Moors

First Published in 2012 on behalf of:
Steven Doherty First Floor Café

Published by:
RMC Books – www.rmcbooks.co.uk

RMC
BOOKS

DEDICATIONS

We would like to dedicate this book to our hard working staff, especially Allan, Sandra, Edel and Cheryl who have been with us from the Café beginning and before; our families who have always been such enthusiastic supporters of everything we've achieved since we've been up in the Lakes; all the people with whom we have shared good company, good food and the odd good bottle or two ... you know who you are!

... and finally, thank you Albert and Sam for your kind words.

menus and what's upstairs

First floor restaurant
Quiet area
Kid's room
Baby change
Toilets

FIRST
FLOOR
AT LAKELAND

If you would like to visit
our Café... Please pop
over and see us at the
information point in store
or in the Café itself.

When our Café is full we will:
• Give you a pager.
• Give you an approximate waiting time.
• Alert you when your table is ready.

If you are part way through your
shopping when you are paged, we will
look after it for you.

IN THE BEGINNING

It's true to say I've worked in some fantastic Michelin-starred restaurants, and alongside some of the modern-day greats. So why write a book about down-to-earth cooking? The answer is simple. I love it.

I developed a taste for basic ingredients when I was quite young – and it has always stayed with me.

I was born in Manchester where my maternal grandmother had a grocery shop. She used to prepare all the food for the shop such as hams and potted meat, but she'd produce meals for us of things such as kidneys, black pudding and tripe. I was eating pigs' trotters when I was three because my grandmother was cooking them and it was a natural part of growing up.

In those days, mothers taught their daughters how to cook and my mother learned from my grandmother how to make wonderful broths, game stews and roasts. She did a lot of her own baking making wonderful bread and scones.

As a boy I enjoyed eating – and watching my grandmother and my mother cook, but I didn't get into it myself.

My family moved to Formby near Liverpool where I was educated. I liked history and art, and did design at evening classes. But I think what inspired me to consider cooking seriously was watching people like Graham Kerr, the Galloping Gourmet, on television. His programme and the approach he took was all very ground breaking. He could cook well and he had a way of captivating the audience. I thought this was amazing; a wonderful skill. Robert Carrier, the American chef, was another one – a very flamboyant character and a great host. Francis Coulson and Brian Sack, who ran Sharrow Bay country house hotel on Lake Ullswater, demonstrated these talents. They were renowned for feeding their guests well in a cocoon of warm hospitality that cosseted and comforted. It's a real skill and something a chef, especially a chef/patron, needs to appreciate if he is to do well in the business.

A somewhat apprehensive Steven Doherty (4th right) is presented to the great and good of Lyon in 1981 by Alain Chapel

I ended up going to college in Southport to do a City and Guilds in basic cookery. I was quite lucky because a man running the course – George Toplis – was a no-nonsense kind of chap. He was a fantastic tutor who taught me about hard work and getting things done.

When I asked his advice about where to go after the course, he bluntly replied: "Go to London, mate." London, after all, was where it was all happening in the mid-1970s and the best training was to be found in a high class hotel. These were times when there wasn't anything like the number and range of restaurants there are in the capital today.

George had contacts in the top 5-star London hotels. At his suggestion, I wrote off to The Savoy, Hilton and Dorchester and was accepted by Silvino Trompetto from The Savoy. Off I went. Most of the hotel kitchens in London were staffed by Northern lads like me, hoping to find their way in the industry – Brian Turner, Marcus Wareing and Paul Heathcote spring to mind.

There were a hundred men in the kitchens at The Savoy and only two women. To say it was a male-dominated environment was putting it mildly.

In my two years there, I realised quite early on that the food wasn't as good as it could be. It was of a good standard and fresh and seasonal, largely made up of typical 5-star restaurant food such as sole Veronique and meat off the trolley. What was missing was a little inspiration.

But it was a great training ground as I was doing everything from breakfasts to banquets and that stays with you forever.

Cheeky young chef gets to work. The photographer caught me preparing for a wine dinner hosted by Albert Roux for the late great Robert Mondavi.

LE GAVROCHE AND THE MICHELIN STARS

In my second year at The Savoy, I decided to enrol at Ealing College on an advanced cookery course. It was there I met an Australian guy working at the Waterside Inn at Bray, owned by the Roux brothers, Michel and Albert, who also had Le Gavroche. It sounded something like the kind of place I'd love to work, so he advised me to write to Albert Roux. I did and was surprised to get a letter back inviting me for an interview.

I was greeted by a diminutive man, dressed in a grey, roll-neck jumper, olive green corduroy trousers and clogs. I'd never seen a picture of Albert Roux – but here was the man himself!

He asked why I wanted a job at Le Gavroche. "I want to learn how to cook properly", I told him.

"Start in September," he said. And that was that.

I walked back to my flat and rang Albert's secretary from the payphone in the hallway.

"Did I really get that job?" I asked, still in a state of shock.

"Yes. Just write back and confirm you're coming," she said.

I found out later that Albert had been impressed because I had wanted to learn.

And so it was I started at Le Gavroche in September 1978 in the tiny basement kitchen of the restaurant's original site in Lower Sloane Street, Chelsea.

I struggled at first. There was a crazy chef called Jean-Louis who was French, the kitchen staff were mainly French, everything to do with the dining room was French, the menus were in French and everyone spoke nothing but French. I was thrown in the deep end but I learned quickly – and it's where I developed my love and understanding of the French language and culture.

Cooking lobsters with Albert. Happy days.

I started off as commis chef in the pastry section and gradually worked my way around, ending up as chef de partie tournant, capable of running all sections.

In the early 1980s, while Le Gavroche was relocating to its current address in Upper Brook Street, Mayfair, Albert sent me to the kitchens of the late Alain Chapel's restaurant in Mionnay, just outside Lyon where I was based for the next two years.

It was during this period that I met up with Marj again. We had known each other since we were 11 when we both attended Formby High School but we had lost touch when we left. I'd come home from Lyon for the Christmas holidays and was out with a group of my friends and bumped into Marj and a group of her friends. We looked at each other and we both thought: "I know you …". We spent the rest of the night chatting and something just clicked.

We arranged to go out for lunch a few days later and ended up in a basement restaurant where I ordered a stew with salad on the side – quite normal in France, but Marj thought it seemed completely loopy to be eating salad on a winter's day in Liverpool.

When I went back to Lyon we wrote to each other practically every day. I proposed over the telephone three months later.

Jean Cocteau
1955

Traditions & Qualité

LES GRANDES TABLES
DU MONDE

Le Gavroche Ltd.

43 Upper Brook Street. London W1

REGISTERED OFFICE

*With my fellow Manchester United fan and friend Michel Roux jnr in London recently.
I seem to recall we were laughing about City's chances of winning the title!*

At the end of 1982 I came back to Le Gavroche as sous chef and Marj skived off her business studies degree course in Manchester and came down to London to join me. We married in August 1983 and this is when Albert Roux introduced us to Sharrow Bay and the Lake District, where we had our honeymoon.

Marj realised that my ambition to one day open my own restaurant meant she would have to get involved and so she started to work for Roux Restaurants. After a time as a waitress at Le Gamin, a basement brasserie just off Fleet Street, she went on to manage Gavvers restaurant, in the building where the original Le Gavroche had been.

At this stage Albert and Michel Snr had several restaurants and contract catering businesses in and around the City. Marj eventually went on to work in the accounts and personnel departments at the head office on Wandsworth Road.

During this period, Le Gavroche was awarded three Michelin star status and in 1985, I became the first British person to become head chef of a three Michelin star establishment. For the next five years, until I left, Le Gavroche won every major European food accolade.

Michel Jnr, Albert's son, took over the day-to-day running of Le Gavroche at the end of 1989, when I was made Group Executive Chef for Roux Restaurants. I was responsible for the existing food operations in three restaurants and ten food and beverage contracts – serving about 3,000 meals a day for everything from directors' boardrooms and Bafta receptions to staff restaurants and sandwich outlets.

It was at this time that I first met and worked with Sue Harrison, who was Group Operations Manager for Roux Restaurants. She is now Director of Catering and Retail Services for the House of Commons and one of the most respected leaders in the catering industry.

In 1991, I became only the fifth British chef to be awarded a Master of Culinary Art – and in the same year, I was asked to be part of Albert Roux's consultancy team that opened The Grand Hotel in Amsterdam. I was only supposed to go for six months, but ended up staying for two years.

THE LAKE DISTRICT BECKONS

What to do after all that? We didn't really want to go back to London, that was for certain. And then luck intervened. I spotted an advert in a catering magazine for a chef partner at the Brown Horse at Winster. Marj and I knew the Lakes from honeymoon and visits to the Sharrow Bay, when we fell in love with the place and often returned over the years.

I recognised the name of the person in the advert – Rudi Schaeffer – as the father of an apprentice I had worked with at Le Gavroche. I rang from Amsterdam and we arranged to meet at the pub. It didn't take long to convince me this was something worth getting involved in.

We signed up. I was in the kitchen and Marj was out the front.

The Brown Horse was a remarkable experience. Even to this day there are pubs that dream of being as busy as we were. The customers came in droves. The food was straightforward, but a far cry from your average pub food. We did kebabs, chicken schnitzel, stuffed cannelloni, houmous and Mediterranean vegetables. We did staple dishes such as steak and kidney pudding and goulash as well, but people loved the variety.

During our tenure, it was voted best pub in the country by both Jonathan Meades of The Times and Emily Green of The Independent.

We didn't want to leave the Brown Horse, but in 1995, we had the chance of buying into the Punch Bowl, two miles down the road at Crosthwaite, then owned by Alan Bell and Lionel Yates. With some financial help from Marj's dad, we took the plunge.

I wanted to produce food based on my classical roots so that meant pork rillettes, French onion soup, duck leg confit and Tarte Tatin, but also traditional British dishes such as braised shoulder of lamb, steak pies and crumbles.

Within 12 months of its opening, the pub was voted Lake District Pub of the Year and ranked as one of the nation's top ten country pubs by Which? magazine. It was also applauded by the judges in the annual Caterer and Hotelkeeper Catey awards. Marj and I were declared winners of the inaugural Pub Operator of the Year in 1997. The Punch Bowl was also voted Cumbria Dining Pub of the Year by the Good Pub Guide three times and I was awarded North West Chef of the Year by Life magazine in 2002.

All in all, we weren't doing too badly!

We were there for ten years and then, as is the way with such things, life took another culinary turn. One day we were out and about in the Lakes and popped in for lunch at the Lakeland shop, then a much smaller place than it is today. The Miller Howe Café was tucked away in a corner. It was a tiny little place of just 14 tables, but the place was packed. The thought occurred to me that I wouldn't mind getting my pinkies on this one day.

Not long afterwards, we were introduced to Julian Rayner of Lakeland. During our chat I made a throwaway remark to the effect that if the opportunity to run the café ever came up… and the seed was sown. Soon afterwards a call came out of the blue from Julian to say he might be looking for someone to take it over. We tendered for it – and the rest, as they say…

In January 2005 we decided to concentrate our energies in the Café and sold the Punch Bowl to a friend and now culinary colleague, Richard Rose.

BEYOND THE LAKES

Over the years I have advised several local businesses to help develop their kitchens. I also spent three years working with Craig Stevenson, of Braehead Foods in Kilmarnock, one of the largest food wholesalers and game processing businesses in Scotland. He wanted to establish a cookery school on the west coast so we set up The Cook School Scotland. There was huge media attention in that venture, not least because we established a private dining scheme at Dumfries House, cooking for exalted guests such as members of the Royal Family.

Several years ago, I got a call out of the blue from Gordon Ramsay who wanted me to help judge the Gordon Ramsay Scholarship in Scotland – and I was chairman of the judges for eight years.

I still have a number of consultancies as well as my work at the First Floor Café.

Following a call from Alex Brodie – founder and managing director of Hawkshead Brewery in Staveley – we created the Beer Kitchen adjacent to the Beer Hall. Alex wanted to do food to go with the amazing selection of beers and we came up with an innovative range of tapas and bite size dishes.

I'm also involved with the Edinburgh New Town Cookery School. Founder and principal Fiona Burrell asked me to develop a masterclass for her students so I go up there about six times a year to work with them. We have also launched Dinner, Demo and Dine evenings there for the general public.

My latest consultancy is in Grasmere with Chris Carrs, who owns and runs the Rothay Garden country house hotel.

I tend to get called on throughout the year to judge various competitions and to speak at chefs' conferences.

The Dorchester

CATERER
AND HOTELKEEPER

SARA JAYNE STANES

MY WAY OF THINKING

What's the difference between a chef and a cook? That's a good question. In our business if you say someone's a great cook it doesn't mean they are an all-round professional. But you need to be a great cook to become a great chef. To become a great chef you need to have leadership, organisation, discipline and structure as well as the culinary skills. You need to know how the business runs; you need to be good with facts and figures.

Importantly, you need to know what customers' needs are. That doesn't mean you have to cater for every obscure dietary need or become known for delivering wacky menus because this will overtake the business you are trying to create. There is a fine line between respecting the customer's wishes and setting your stall out.

My principles definitely lie in not only using seasonal food – that is one of the crucial things for me – but also bringing flavours out and just giving people real honest food. That's it.

We will put John Stott's sausages in a baguette with fried onions and serve that any day of the year but in winter we will use some of his game, including estate-shot venison, in a pie or casserole. But whatever we use, it will be fresh and in season. We are not going to serve tomato soup in December or asparagus in January.

I enjoy coming up with creative ideas for food and I'm inspired by all sorts, including cookery writers in the weekend newspapers and magazines, who give me some great ideas.

Foremost among them is Diana Henry, of The Sunday Telegraph magazine, whose key works include a number of outstanding cookery books and she also wrote the two gastropub cookbooks, in which we featured.

In the café when I'm developing dishes it is important to involve the head chef and senior staff.

When I eat out and come across dishes that excite me, I'll think how ingredients can be incorporated to enhance the café menu – you have to keep an eye on what's happening and keep tailoring the business.

ALBERT ROUX

Albert Roux was born in 1935 at Semur-en-Brionnais in the region of Saone et Loire in France. The family were charcutiers so it's hardly surprising Albert – and his brother Michel – went into the food industry.

Albert started his career as an apprentice patissier but went on to cook for wealthy individuals including Lady Nancy Astor at her country home at Cliveden, and at the French Embassy in London and the British Embassy in Paris.

He spent eight years working as a chef for the Cazalet family at their estate in Kent and it was during this time he was encouraged to open his own restaurant, which he did with Michel in 1967. It was Le Gavroche, where I first went to work with him.

When I first started I was out of my depth and had to work incredibly hard. Albert is a very kind man but a great taskmaster. However, I had a strong mental resolve and I knew I was going to make it no matter what. I had this mantra that nothing would get to me; I would just carry on and work hard no matter what was thrown at me – and it paid dividends. I think Albert appreciates that sort of resolve in a person. He puts a lot of effort into training and his chefs are prepared to give a lot of effort back.

The Roux brothers opened the Waterside Inn at Bray in 1972 and they also started a catering service, as well as opening more restaurants and brasseries in London, including Le Gamin and Gavvers.

Michel eventually took over the Waterside and it was Albert's son, Michel Jnr, who took over Le Gavroche while his father explored other avenues such as creating the Albert Roux Consultancy, which has advised on the setting-up and running of a series of restaurants and hotels around the world.

"ALBERT APPRECIATES
RESOLVE IN A PERSON.
HE PUTS A LOT OF EFFORT
INTO TRAINING AND HIS
CHEFS REPAY THAT WITH
HARD WORK."

Albert is supremely well respected within the catering industry but he's a bonkers 77-year-old with the energy of a 50-year-old and is forever wanting to do other things! When I was at Le Gavroche he said that he didn't want to end his days in the kitchen but he just loves what he does; he's just one of those guys who keeps going on.

The Roux brothers were pioneers in the way they introduced fine dining in Britain and they have won countless awards both here and in France – not least those Michelin stars – and Albert has been awarded both the OBE and the Legion d'Honneur.

Albert nurtured me, but he was also an inspiration to many other young chefs who have made it in the business, not least Paul Rankin, Rowley Leigh, Marcus Wareing, Pierre Koffmann, Marco Pierre White and Gordon Ramsay.

I owe him a great debt and we remain firm friends to this day. We often meet socially, but he is the first person with whom I would discuss any aspect of the business because I value and respect what he has to say.

HOME IN THE LAKES

The Lake District feels like home.

We live in a wonderful Victorian three-storey terrace house with views over the Langdale Pikes from one window and Orrest Head (784 feet high) from another. We feel incredibly settled.

You can never take the Lakes for granted – there are so many wonderful places and stunning views.

One of our favourite walks is along to the Watermill at Ings. We amble over there, have lunch and amble back. We also like the climb and view from Gummers Howe and then a restorative beverage at the Masons Arms at Strawberry Bank, overlooking the Winster Valley. There are fabulous views at every point of the compass from here, not least that which looks out to Morecambe Bay.

We eat out several times a month. There's a good Italian fairly close by as well as a Chinese and some really good pubs and restaurants, which do a range of food from traditional to contemporary and quirky.

At home, Marj enjoys baking while I make most of our meals. My philosophy is that you are what you eat and that what you eat should be healthy and it should do you good. So we have lots of salads, homemade broths, fish, white meat dishes, pasta and fresh vegetables in the main. A treat might be a huge steak, which we share.

We love entertaining and have made some close friends since we moved to the Lakes. And, luckily, they love good food and wine.

OUR FRIENDS IN THE LAKES

My suppliers are incredibly important to me because without the right suppliers a chef is nothing.

I look for the same values in all of them: integrity, quality and reliability. And they've got to have consistency in the service, the product and the delivery.

Because I have lived and worked in the Lakes for several years, I've learned who is good and who has the best reputation. It's vital to know what's going on.

You might get to know a supplier through word of mouth, but generally, you look at who else they are supplying. The best are always supplying the top end of the market and I use people who are doing that.

It's important also to support people when they are starting out in business and I have done that with some of my suppliers. I'm happy to support them because it's something I have always thought: if you look after them, they will look after you.

It's also crucial to support suppliers based in Cumbria and who are serving the Cumbrian market. I'm not going to use a butcher in Liverpool – I'm going to support local people and the local economy.

But my ongoing relationship is crucial – I never let them get too cosy and if things are not right I will tell them.

PATRICK MORE

Patrick More at More Artisan is a neighbour of Alex's at the Mill Yard in Staveley. He started off working in a restaurant kitchen after school when he was only a young lad – doing vegetable prep and clearing up. One day, the chef didn't turn up and because he'd been watching what went on, Patrick offered to do the cooking. How great was that? Getting paid to play with fire!

He's a real worker – as well as the kitchen job, he had a milk round and a paper round. He'd clear snow for people in the winter and do some landscape gardening in the summer.

Eventually he quit the odd jobs and went to college before moving into full-time catering.

He's always been interested in breadmaking and is a campaigner for real bread. He strongly believes that the proper stuff should taste of something.

His bakery was born when he knocked three rooms into one at his home in Kendal to give him a little elbow-room for serious baking.

He started out producing about 20 loaves and 30 tarts a day but the business grew and bigger premises were needed. Now he makes a continually-evolving range of artisan breads by the ton. And he uses only natural ingredients and traditional slow fermentation methods.

He has gone from strength to strength. He is very shrewd, and no slouch. He's not frightened to ruffle feathers and that's one of the reasons I wanted to support him. He will stick his neck out for something he believes in.

MŎRE? THE ARTISAN BAKER

Cheddar & Onion
Ciabatta Rolls
75p

MŎRE?

ALEX BRODIE

When I got involved with Hawkshead Brewery it was a business that was growing rapidly; a business with a real solid base and one that had integrity. Alex Brodie, who owns it, was a foreign correspondent for the BBC who covered events around the world, but he always had a real passion for beer.

He founded the brewery in 2002 in a 17th century barn at the head of Esthwaite Water, just outside Hawkshead and it grew so quickly that four years later, it relocated to larger premises at the Mill Yard, Staveley. Alex installed a new brewery and developed The Beer Hall – a showcase for real ale.

The core range of beers, which includes Windermere Pale, Hawkshead Bitter, Red, Lakeland Gold and Brodie's Prime, are now benchmark standard in the industry. When I taste beer, Alex's are always the barometer because they are so good and so well made.

Alex rang me out of the blue in October 2010. He knew of my reputation and had also heard I had done some consulting. We met and he told me he had decided to start serving food but knew it was stepping outside his beer comfort zone. I liked the business and got on board. We fitted out the kitchen and I brought in the chef, Kester Marsh. We developed the menus and the Beer Kitchen was created. It specialises in tapas and other small dishes – all of them delicious and inexpensive – and specifically designed to complement the beer.

HAWKSH

BREWERS OF TRADITIONAL

ENTRA

BAR OP

12 NOON

EAD BREWERY

EERS WITH A MODERN TWIST SINCE 2002

NCE

THE BEER HALL

PETER & FRANCES FRYER

Peter and Frances Fryer deliberately spent a lot of time looking for the right food business to take over. They were determined that whatever they were going to do, it needed to be special. It came in the shape of English Lakes Ice Cream.

At the time, it was a tiny business running out of an old engine shed in the Lake District village of Burneside. They sold everything to buy the business and get it up and running how they wanted it. Soon it was producing about 60,000 litres of ice cream a year. Even their children were involved in making it.

They have since moved to bigger premises at the Old Dairy, just outside Kendal, from where three-quarter of a million litres of ice cream and sorbets is now made each year in a comprehensive range of flavours. The products are sold throughout the Lake District, up into the Scottish borders and down as far as Manchester.

It's still a compact business, with five staff on the manufacturing side, four on distribution and Peter and Frances doing all the admin and sales. But what's important to me is that they have remained true to their values and core strengths. In an ideal world, we would make our own ice cream at the café. We don't because English Lakes is so hard to beat.

SIMON THOMAS

Another artisan baker that we use is Simon Thomas who runs the Staff of Life. He's an amazing guy who operates from a tiny bakery/shop in Kendal – and he does what he does very well. He's quirky and innovative, a very natural guy and at ease with himself.

His grandmother taught him how to make bread when he was very young and the enthusiasm continued as he grew up. It was a skill that was to come in useful at university. A particularly happy arrangement with two other student friends developed. While Simon contributed the bread, one made wine and the other had the knack of cooking perfect chips. Between them they had the best chip butty suppers in town!

Simon and his wife Julie started the Staff of Life in 1997 and now produce anything from 200 loaves a day, as well as cakes, gingerbread and tarts.

They are driven by a quest for taste and the secret of their bread is to use first-rate ingredients, then blend them prior to a long fermentation to extract the full flavour.

The range is under constant development, driven by Simon's imagination. But whatever he bakes, his bread is always full of texture and taste. As Simon himself says, why bother with white, sliced when you can have real bread?

STAFF LIFE
OF
Artisan Bakery
Handmade filled
and flavoured loaf

Staff of Life

Real Artisan Bread

01539 738606

Omega
Wholemeal
Tin
£1-60

VIKI POWELL

We've been using Farrer's since we came to the Lakes.

The company dates back to 1819 when John Farrer started the family business as a specialist tea and coffee merchant. Farrers now import Arabica coffee beans which are roasted in their own factory on the outskirts of Kendal.

Everyone who works there is passionate about what they do. The company is run by Viki Powell, aided by a team of staff. Many of the coffee blends were developed by her late husband, Richard, who could claim 50 years experience in the business.

It's not a small set up, but they still manage to retain the personal touch.

JONATHAN & SUSAN STOTT

Jonathan Stott, at Cartmel Valley Game Supplies, is a larger-than-life character. He's an amiable guy with a business of really high quality. A former head keeper on a local estate, he started the business with his wife, Susan in 1993, in a 17th century farmhouse. They source game, such as venison, pheasant, pigeon and rabbit from local shoots. Their line of smoked items, which includes meat, fish and poultry, is excellent and, again, it's all processed on the premises in the lovely Cartmel Valley.

The Stotts supply the top end of the market, including Michelin starred restaurants. The fact that his products are smoked locally over beech wood, I'm reliably informed, just adds to the value.

Claire's Handmade
Old Fashioned
Plum Chutney
The classic English chutney,
perfect with a cheese board!

Claire's Handmade
Apricot & Apple
Chutney
Sweet and Spicy – that'll do nicely!

Claire's Handmade
Hot Lemon Relish
with Harissa Spices
Piquant, zesty,
enticing and hot!

Claire's Handmade
Lakel...
Farmh...
Chu...
Gently spiced T...
Chutney – a sa...

CLAIRE KENT

If you want amazing preserves and chutneys, you need to know about Claire's Handmade. It's run by Claire Kent and her husband, Michael. The two of them have always been involved in catering, but they decided to branch into this specialist area. Their products are made in the kitchen of their home in a small village near Wigton, using Claire's mother's treasured Aga jam pan. They initially sold the produce at local shows and farmers' markets, but as the business grew the time came to move to a bigger base in Wigton itself, complete with a purpose-built kitchen.

They come up with lots of new and innovative ideas for savoury and sweet jams, chutneys, piccalillis and marmalades and they've won numerous awards.

All the products are made in the traditional way from traditional recipes and there are no artificial ingredients.

There are other producers out there but I particularly like what Claire does and the style of everything she produces. I have stuck with her because she has retained the insistence on quality that I look for.

"Thank goodness for eggs"

FRESH EGGS
30 DOZEN

JOHN
ATKINSON

I am passionate about fresh eggs. I get mine from John Atkinson, who farms at Underbarrow, near Kendal. His family have been selling eggs for a hundred years so it's a well established, local business.

I like to buy straight from the farm. I can always tell they are fresh because when you crack them the yolk really sits up and the white will be half an inch high – the older the egg is, the more likely that the albumen turns to water and runs off.

We can use 100 eggs a day here at the café, so it's important every one of them is fresh.

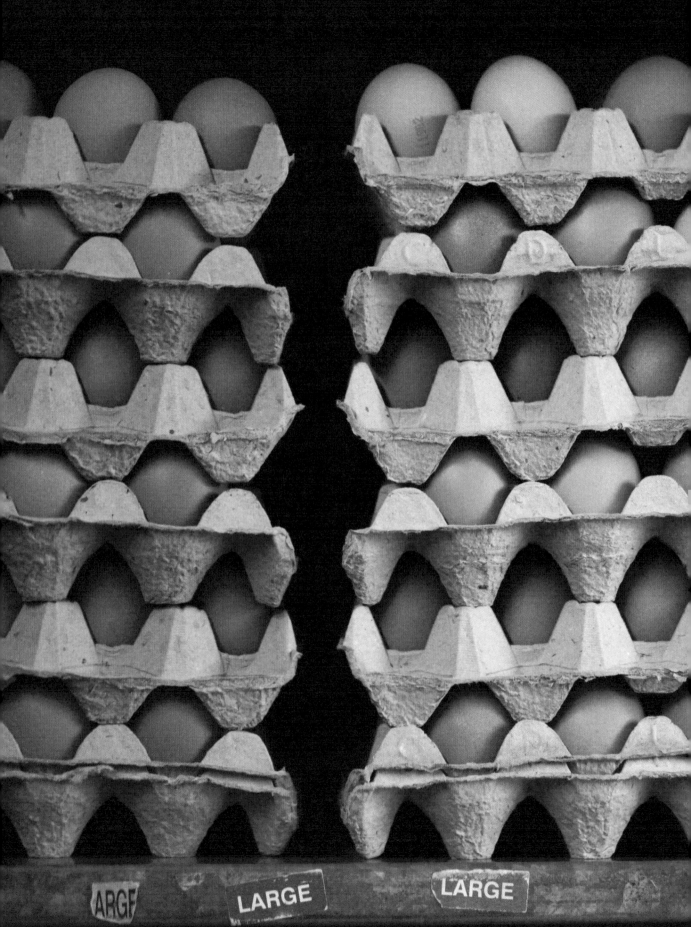

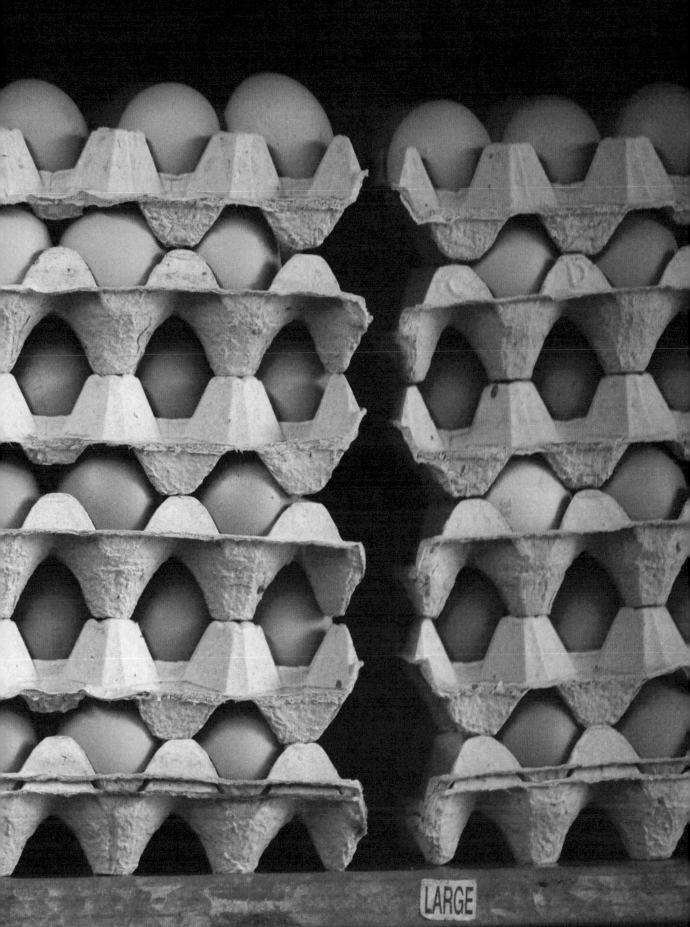

LARGE

BAKED JACKET POTATO WITH A SMOKED HADDOCK & CREAMY LEEK SAUCE

INGREDIENTS – SERVES 4

4 large size baking potatoes

4 medium eggs

2 x 800g naturally smoked haddock fillets

100ml white wine

500ml double cream

1 large leek, split lengthways, washed and finely shredded

1 dessertspoon onion, finely diced

2 dessertspoons Dijon mustard

1 dessertspoon grain mustard

100g Parmesan cheese, grated

150ml milk

1 litre water

METHOD

Preheat the oven to 180ºC.

Scrub and wrap the potatoes in foil and bake for about 75-90 minutes.

Poach the eggs. (See method below).

Put the onions and white wine in a saucepan, set on a gentle heat and reduce by half.

Add the cream and bring to a simmer.

Stir in the leek and cook for a further 2-3 minutes, then season lightly.

Fill a large saucepan with the water, add the milk and bring to a simmer.

Add the haddock and poach for 6 minutes.

Cut the baked potatoes in half lengthways, fork them and keep hot. (Alternatively serve on mashed potato).

Drain the fish, allow to cool slightly then peel off the skin and remove any small bones.

Place a small pan of lightly salted water on to boil. Reheat the poached eggs for 4 minutes.

Add the flaked fish to the sauce.

Spoon over the jacket halves, sprinkle with Parmesan cheese and brown under a hot grill.

Drain the eggs onto a clean tea towel and place on top of the potatoes.

POACHED EGGS

Fill a large saucepan three quarters full with water and add a good 250ml of distilled vinegar. Bring to a boil – DO NOT ADD SALT.

Break 6 large super fresh eggs into individual tea cups. (Always add an extra 2 so that you will get 4 perfect ones.)

Gently tip the eggs into the boiling water, put a lid on and bring back to a simmer. The eggs will have risen to the surface. Cook for 3-4 minutes.

Remove carefully with a slotted spoon and place into a bowl of iced water. Allow the eggs to settle for at least 5 minutes.

Remove carefully and trim with a small sharp knife to remove any "frilly edges". Keep refrigerated in a sealed container on a clean tea towel. The eggs will keep for 2-3 days.

CULLEN SKINK

INGREDIENTS – SERVES 4-6

125g smoked haddock fillet per person, skinned and boned by fishmonger

125g Savoy cabbage, quartered, washed and finely sliced

125g leeks, split lengthways, washed and finely sliced

2 large potatoes (choose a variety suitable for mashing, eg: Red Roosters) washed, peeled and each cut into 6 even pieces

125ml milk

1litre water

2 soupspoons onion, finely diced

Salt and ground white pepper

Parsley to garnish, chopped or picked

METHOD

Put the potatoes into a pan of cold water with a teaspoon of salt, bring to a simmer and allow to cook for 15 minutes.

In a large pan add the litre of cold water, the milk and onion and bring to a simmer.

Add the fish and cook for 5 minutes.

Remove the fish with a slotted spoon onto a clean plate, cover with cling film and keep warm.

Add the leeks and cabbage to the cooking liquid and cook for a further 7 minutes.

Drain the potatoes and mash until smooth.

Stir in mash to the leeks and cabbage – enough to thicken the broth.

Taste for seasoning. You may need to add a little pepper but probably no salt.

TO SERVE – 2 WAYS

1. Flake the haddock and stir into the broth OR

2. Put the haddock into a deep soup plate and pour the broth over it.

To make it extra special top the dish with a soft-poached egg. (See page 89)

DO IT YOUR WAY

If you want the skink to stick to your ribs just add more mashed potato.

Arbroath Smokies could also be used. For a touch of luxury, stir in a little finely sliced smoked salmon at the last minute.

FISHCAKES

INGREDIENTS – MAKES 8 SMALL OR 4 LARGE FISHCAKES

2 large pre-cooked baked potatoes – Red Roosters are particularly good if you can find them

200g salmon

200g white fish such as whiting, coley or pollack

Splash white wine

2 dessertspoons onion, chopped

2 dessertspoons parsley, chopped

25g unsalted butter

100g Greenland prawns

Plain flour

Sunflower oil

METHOD

Pre-heat the oven to 180°C.

Scoop out the potatoes and mash well with a potato masher.

Cook the fish with the onion, white wine and butter until flaky. (Approximately 10 minutes).

Drain and allow to cool.

Mix together the potato and the fish and prawns. When combined, add the parsley.

Shape into the required size of cakes.

Heat a 30cm non-stick frying pan and add a splash of oil.

Lightly dust the cakes with flour and cook on both sides until golden.

Place on a baking tray and finish cooking in the oven for approximately 8-10 minutes to ensure they are cooked through.

TO SERVE

A poached egg finishes the dish off perfectly. Serve with a side salad or vegetables with some tartare sauce.

AS YOU LIKE IT

The great thing about this ever-popular dish is that you can tweak it to your liking. Use a mixture of more salmon and less white fish or vice versa, according to your preference. No need to stop there – why not mussells, smoked fish or even crab? It's easy to add oriental or spicy flavours with a little finely-chopped spring onion, coriander, or chilli .

LAKELAND
the home of creative kitchenware™

Use a good non-stick frying pan (ref.13676)
with a silicon fish slice (ref.11561).

GOAT'S CHEESE SALAD

INGREDIENTS – SERVES 4

4 slices goat's cheese log, rind removed

4 slices rye bread or sourdough

32 frozen button onions, defrosted or 8 spring onions, finely sliced

250g packet of 4 pre-cooked beetroot, each cut into 6 wedges

25g unsalted butter

Mixed salad leaves of your choice – include rocket and radicchio for some bite

Virgin olive oil

Good quality balsamic vinegar

Salt and freshly ground pepper

Sunflower oil

Pinch of sugar

METHOD

Heat a splash of sunflower oil in a pan with the butter add the onions and sugar then fry until golden brown. Season lightly.

Place the goat's cheese slices on top of the bread, brush lightly with sunflower oil and grill until golden.

Add the beetroot to the onions or simply grill with the goat's cheese to warm the beetroot.

Lightly toss the salad leaves with a good splash of olive oil and balsamic vinegar.

TO SERVE

Arrange the salad leaves on individual plates and place the goat's cheese on top.

Scatter the beetroot and onions around the leaves.

Lightly toss the salad leaves with a good splash of olive oil and balsamic vinegar in a large salad bowl (ref.15709)

HOME-CURED GRAVAD LAX WITH A SWEET GRAIN MUSTARD RELISH

INGREDIENTS – SERVES 10

FOR THE SALMON

50g whole white peppercorns

50g dried dill weed

50g caster sugar

1kg coarse sea salt

2kg fully trimmed side of salmon, boned and skinned

25g Dijon mustard

FOR THE RELISH

100g Dijon mustard

100g grain mustard

65g caster sugar

10g dried dill weed

A splash white wine vinegar to taste

A dribble of sunflower oil (or a little more until the relish is the consistency of runny honey)

METHOD

Coarsely grind the peppercorns, then mix together with the sugar, salt and half the dill.

Put the salmon in a deep tray and cover both sides with the salt mixture.

Cover and leave in a cold place for 24 hours.

Remove the salmon from the salt mixture and rinse under cold running water.

Dry the salmon on a wire tray in a cold place for 48 hours.

On a piece of greaseproof paper, coat the non-skin side of the salmon with Dijon mustard and the remainder of the dried dill.

Shake off the excess dill and keep it to use another time.

Store the salmon in a cold place for 24 hours. (It can, if necessery be used immediately.)

FOR THE RELISH

Mix all the ingredients together, put into an airtight container and refrigerate – will keep for 1 month.

TO SERVE

Slice thinly. Refrigerated it will keep well for 2 weeks.

The relish can be kept in these clip top Kilner preserving jars. (ref.16229)

GRILLED MACKEREL FILLETS BOIS BOUDRAN

This is one of the Roux's all-time favourite sauces – and surely one of the few French recipes that calls for tomato ketchup!

INGREDIENTS – SERVES 4

4 prepared mackerel fillets

Sunflower oil

Cracked black pepper

1 teaspoon chives, chopped

200ml virgin olive oil

2 dessertspoons white wine vinegar

2 shakes Worcestershire sauce

FOR THE BOIS BOUDRAN SAUCE

1 teaspoon parsley, chopped

1 teaspoon tarragon, chopped

1 teaspoon chervil, chopped

1 dessertspoon tomato ketchup

2 teaspoon shallots, finely chopped

Pinch salt

METHOD

Brush the mackerel fillets with a little sunflower oil.

Season lightly with salt and pepper and grill lightly on both sides or pan-fry in a non-stick pan.

FOR THE BOIS BOUDRAN SAUCE

Mix together the oil, tomato ketchup, white wine vinegar and Worcestershire sauce.

Add the herbs and shallots and check the seasoning.

TO SERVE

Mix together some salad leaves, including rocket and watercress for a bit of bite. Divide the salad onto 4 plates.

Place a mackerel fillet on top of the salad and spoon the sauce around it.

the home of creative kitchenware™

A hard anodised non-stick frying pan is essential (ref.13676) with a sturdy flat fish slice to remove the mackerel (ref.11555)

HASHCAKES WITH ONION GRAVY

INGREDIENTS – MAKES 4 CAKES

FOR THE HASHCAKES

2 large pre-cooked baked potatoes – Red Roosters are good

198g tin corned beef, mashed up

4 dessertspoons onion, chopped

2 dessertspoons parsley, chopped

150ml pre-made onion gravy (see recipe)

Plain flower

Sunflower oil

4 medium size free-range eggs

FOR THE ONION GRAVY

4 large white onions, peeled and thinly sliced

500ml dry white wine

1 litre good beef stock in vac-pac pouches from a good supermarket – True Foods for example

Salt and freshly ground black pepper

50g unsalted butter

2 dessertspoons sugar

METHOD

Pre-heat the oven to 180ºC.

Scoop out the potatoes and mash well with a potato masher.

Mix the potato with the corned beef, onions and parsley.

Shape into 4 large cakes.

Heat a large frying pan with an ovenproof handle and add a good splash of oil.

Lightly dust the cakes with flour and cook on both sides until golden.

Finish cooking in the oven for 10 minutes.

Fry the eggs in small non-stick frying pans.

TO SERVE

Pour a pool of gravy onto a plate.

Carefully place a hashcake on the gravy and slide a fried egg on top.

FOR THE ONION GRAVY

In a thick-bottomed sauce pan melt the butter, add the onions and sweat without any colour for approximately 25 minutes.

Add the sugar and the white wine and cook until reduced by a quarter.

Add the stock, bring to a simmer and cook slowly until reduced by half.

Taste and adjust seasoning if necessary.

This can be made days ahead and stored in the fridge in jars or sealed containers.

ALTERNATIVELY...

Red wine or beer could be used instead of white wine.

The sugar is an important addition as it balances the acidity of the sauce and brings out the flavour of the onions.

LAKELAND
the home of creative kitchenware™

Lakeland Ceramica single-size frying pans are great for cooking individual fried eggs. (ref.14848)

PEA & HAM SOUP

INGREDIENTS – SERVES 4

1 bacon knuckle

3 sticks celery, washed, 1 left whole and 2 roughly chopped

2 small onions, peeled, 1 left whole and 1 roughly chopped

1 carrot

50g butter

250g green split peas

1.75 litre ham stock

2 bay leaves

1 teaspoon garlic, finely chopped

Pinch salt and ground white pepper

METHOD

Place the knuckle in a deep pan, cover with cold water, then bring to a simmer and skim.

Add 1 whole stick of celery, 1 whole onion, 1 carrot and 1 bay leaf, bring back to a simmer and cook for about 2 hours 30 minutes.

Remove the knuckle and allow to cool. Remove any fat and sinew then cut into strips or dice.

Put the remaining chopped onion and celery into a food processor and blitz to a fine pulp.

Heat a large thick-bottomed pan and melt the butter.

Add the celery and onion pulp and sweat, without colour, for 4-5 minutes.

Stir in the peas and continue sweating for 3-4 minutes.

Add the stock, bay leaves, garlic and white pepper.

Bring to the boil then simmer for 2 hours 30 minutes until the peas are cooked. Remove the bay leaves.

For a smooth soup, place in a liquidiser or use a stick blender. Alternatively, if you prefer a chunkier texture, the soup is now ready to be served.

TO SERVE

Garnish with strips or dice of ham taken from the cooked knuckle.

STOCK ANSWERS

You can make the stock the day before so that the flavours really come through. For those who don't like garlic, it can easily be omitted from the ingredients list without spoiling the end result.

Served in ivory coloured bowls from the Delicious range.
(ref.15675)

SALMON & FENNEL SALAD

INGREDIENTS – SERVES 4

4 x 125g salmon fillets

1 head fennel

1 small red onion, peeled

Mixed salad leaves of your choice – include watercress
and rocket to give some bite

Good quality virgin olive oil

Aged balsamic vinegar

Salt and freshly ground black pepper

Sunflower oil

METHOD

Trim the fennel and shave paper-thin. Do the same with the red onion.

Heat a 30cm non-stick frying pan and add 1 dessertspoon of oil.

Add the salmon fillets and cook on both sides until golden brown, about 8-10 minutes.

Season very lightly in the pan.

Toss the salad leaves with a little olive oil and vinegar.

TO SERVE

Arrange the salad in individual bowls and place a salmon fillet on top.

CONJUGATE THE HERB

You can add some finely-chopped fresh herbs such as mint or tarragon to the salad and if the mood takes you, serve
warm new potatoes or pasta with it. I can't stress enough how important it is to use top quality oil and vinegar – the dish
just isn't the same with anything less.

Presented in individual Acacia wood bowls (ref.15710)

SALMON & MUSHROOM BRUSCHETTA

INGREDIENTS – SERVES 4

8 large field mushrooms

4 long slices of sourdough or sliced ciabatta

4 x 100g salmon fillets

Rocket salad

32 sun-blushed tomatoes

Virgin olive oil

Maldon sea salt

Good balsamic vinegar

Ground black pepper

Sunflower oil

METHOD

Preheat the oven to 180ºC.

Quickly pan-fry the mushrooms in a little sunflower oil. Season with sea salt and pepper.

Toast the bread. Place 2 mushrooms on each slice and allow the juices to soak in.

Heat a large non-stick frying pan and add a splash of sunflower oil.

Season the salmon lightly on both sides with salt and pepper and cook for 2 minutes each side.

Place the salmon on top of the mushrooms and bake in the oven for 5 minutes.

TO SERVE

Lightly dress the rocket with a little olive oil and balsamic vinegar and put on individual plates.

Place the bruschetta on top of each plate and scatter the tomatoes around.

INVEST IN THE BEST

Sun-blushed tomatoes are readily available on most deli counters in good supermarkets and independent delis.

Balsamic vinegar is only as good as the price dictates. Decent bottles start at £18 and go up from there!

LAKELAND

the home of creative kitchenware™

We serve ours on a solid Acacia wood chopping board (ref.15706) with a drizzle of oil. (ref.14090)

SALMON RILLETTES

500g salmon fillet, freshly poached

100ml dry white wine

250g unsalted butter, softened

100ml double cream

2 shallots, finely chopped

Pinch fresh thyme, chopped

Pinch ground black pepper

Pinch grated nutmeg

Pinch cayenne pepper

1 dessertspoon chives, chopped

390g tin red peppers, drained and diced

Juice of 1 lemon

1 dessertspoon tinned green peppercorns

Zest of 1 small orange

Salt to taste

METHOD

Poach the salmon fillet in lightly salted water with the white wine.

When still slightly warm, flake the fish. Add the butter and cream and mix thoroughly.

Add all of the remaining ingredients and taste for seasoning.

Roll in cling film or mould in a cling-filmed lined terrine.

Put into the fridge and leave for at least 12 hours before serving.

TO SERVE

Bring to room temperature before serving.

Great eaten on its own or with sharp relishes or chutneys, sour cream, tzatziki and some toasted granary bread.

SUCCESS ON A PLATE

This is an easy pre-prepared starter for a dinner party or buffet, but it is just at home at a barbecue or picnic.

Other herbs can be used such as sage, parsley or hyssop.

LAKELAND
the home of creative kitchenware™

Serve this with a selection of relishes and chutneys, presented in an attractive serving set for that added wow factor. (ref.13313)

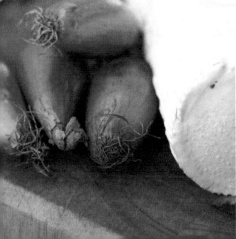

SHALLOT & GOAT'S CHEESE "TARTE TATIN"

Traditionally, Tarte Tatin is a caramelised upside down apple tart. We have taken the concept and added goat's cheese and shallots instead.

INGREDIENTS – MAKES 4 TARTS

12 large banana shallots peeled and cut in half lengthways

1 teaspoon caster sugar

100ml balsamic vinegar

2 sheets pre-rolled Jus Rol puff pastry

Olive oil

400g crumbly goat's cheese, preferably a French goat log

Salt and freshly ground black pepper

EQUIPMENT

4 x 12cm non-stick blini pans or frying pans

METHOD

Put the shallots in a shallow saucepan. Cover with water, add a pinch of salt, sugar and balsamic vinegar and cook very slowly until tender (about 45 minutes).

The liquid should be golden and syrupy. Allow to cool.

Meanwhile, preheat the oven to 180°C.

Cut the pastry into circles, 1cm bigger than the size of the pans.

Lightly brush the pans with olive oil, add the shallots and the remaining reduced syrup then top with the pastry.

Carefully tuck the pastry in and around the shallots to create an edge or crust.

Bake for 12 minutes.

Carefully de-mould the tarts onto a tray.

Top with the cheese, then return to the oven for 5-7 minutes until the cheese is melted and golden.

LAKELAND
the home of creative kitchenware™

Plate from the Delicious Mint range. (ref.15674)

SMOKED SALMON & LEEK QUICHE

INGREDIENTS – MAKES 1 X 30CM X 20CM FLAN TIN

1 packet pre-rolled short crust pastry

1 pint double cream

4 whole medium eggs

5 medium egg yolks

100g Parmesan cheese, grated

Pinch of cayenne pepper

Pinch of ground or freshly grated nutmeg

Sunflower oil

1 large leek, split lengthways, washed and finely sliced

250g pre-sliced smoked salmon, chopped

Salt and freshly ground black pepper

METHOD

Pre-heat the oven to 150ºC.

Line the tin with the pastry ensuring it is well pushed into the edges and leave 2cm overhanging.

Line with greaseproof paper and fill with baking beans. Bake blind for about 30 minutes.

Remove from the oven and allow to cool.

Increase the oven temperature to 165ºC.

Mix together the cream, eggs, 4 egg yolks and Parmesan cheese.

Add the cayenne, nutmeg, a tiny pinch of salt and strain (to ensure there is no shell and also this helps to break the eggs up).

Heat a splash of oil in a thick-bottomed pan, add the leek and sweat without colour for 5 minutes.

Season lightly, allow to cool, then add to the cream mixture. Mix in the smoked salmon.

Remove the beans and paper from the pastry base.

Ensure the base is free from any holes and gaps or fill with pieces of spare pastry.

Beat the remaining egg yolk, brush the base and return to the oven for about 2 minutes – this will help seal the pastry.

Pour the mixture into the pastry. Return to the oven and cook for 1 hour.

Allow the quiche to rest for at least 30-45 minutes before removing from the mould.

For best results, you will need a good quality
30cm x 20cm flan tin. (ref.12508)

SMOOTH CHICKEN LIVER PARFAIT

INGREDIENTS – SERVES 15

600g trimmed chicken livers

600g double cream

3 whole medium eggs

Half teaspoon salt

1 teaspoon pink salt

Half teaspoon chopped garlic

Pinch ground white pepper

Pinch ground nutmeg

METHOD

Preheat the oven to 150ºC.

Blend the chicken livers in a food processor.

Add the eggs and blend together.

Add all the seasonings, garlic and cream.

Blend for 2 minutes.

Strain through a **fine** sieve or chinois.

Pour into a buttered terrine with lid on, and bake for 1 hour 5 minutes.

If the terrine has not fully set, check every 5 minutes to see if it's ready.

Cool as quickly as possible and refrigerate for 24 hours before serving.

Heat the outside of the terrine before de-moulding.

FOR THE PERFECT PARFAIT

It's best to chill the terrine before buttering. But use just enough butter to cover the terrine – don't overdo it.

Keep covered in the fridge and it will last for 3-4 days de-moulded.

The inside will be lovely, smooth and **pink.**

Pink salt is a preservative, if you speak nicely to your butcher he might sell you some.

SMOKED SALMON BLINIS

INGREDIENTS – SERVES 4

FOR THE BLINIS

150g top-quality stoneground wholemeal flour

7g sachet dried yeast

Salt

Pinch of sugar

2 medium eggs, beaten

400ml milk, warmed

4 medium egg whites

Sunflower oil

Unsalted butter

FOR THE TOPPING

4 slices smoked salmon

Savruga caviar

Cream cheese

Dill

METHOD

Preheat the oven to 200°C.

Put the flour into a large bowl and add the dried yeast, a pinch of salt and sugar. Mix well. Add the eggs and milk and mix together.

Cover the bowl with cling film and allow to rise to almost double in size in a warm place.

Beat the egg whites with a pinch of salt until just firm.

Carefully fold the whites bit by bit into the flour mixture.

Preheat individual non-stick pans and add a teaspoon of oil and a half teaspoon of butter.

Drop 2 dessertspoons of the mixture into each pan, cook for 2-3 minutes until set then bake in the oven for 4 minutes, flip over and bake the other side for a further 2 minutes. Repeat.

Allow to cool.

TO SERVE

Spread the blinis with cream cheese, dress with the salmon and top with caviar or dill.

CUTTING COMMENTS

The blinis can be made hours ahead and warmed through.

Small ones are ideal for canapés. Use a 30cm frying pan to make one large blini and cut the required number out with a small straight-sided cutter.

If you are a coeliac or wheat intolerant, buckwheat flour can be used which is a member of the rhubarb family. This is what the traditional Russian blinis were made from.

As well as being perfect for eggs, Lakeland Ceramica single-size frying pans are great for cooking these blinis. (ref.14848)

FILLET OF SALMON WITH STEAMED MUSSELS IN A CREAMY CURRIED SAFFRON SAUCE

INGREDIENTS – SERVES 4

1kg mussels in the shell, scrubbed and bearded

2 dessertspoons onion, finely chopped

1 dessertspoon mild curry powder

175ml dry white wine

4 x 150g salmon fillets

Sunflower oil

1 pinch fresh saffron

300ml double cream

Salt and freshly ground white pepper

2 dessertspoons parsley, chopped (optional)

METHOD

Put the mussels into a large saucepan with the onion, curry powder and wine.

Place on a high heat with the lid on, bring to a boil, reduce to a simmer and cook for 3 minutes.

Meanwhile, season the salmon fillets on both sides.

Heat a 28cm non-stick frying pan, add a splash of sunflower oil and cook the salmon until golden brown on both sides (about 8-10 minutes in total). Keep warm.

Place the mussels into a colander over a bowl and allow to drain for 2-3 minutes.

Put the juices back into the pan, add the saffron then reduce the liquid by half over a moderate heat.

Add the cream and reduce by half again. Taste for seasoning.

Make sure the mussels are open and discard any that remain closed.

Return to the sauce and gently reheat.

TO SERVE

Ladle mussels and sauce into deep bowls, top with salmon and sprinkle with parsley.

LAKELAND
the home of creative kitchenware™

A traditional enamel roaster is ideal to serve from. (ref.13262)

BELLY PORK WITH BLACK PUDDING AND MASHED POTATO

INGREDIENTS – SERVES 10

3kg piece of rolled belly pork, skin on

2 litre duck fat

1 head garlic, whole and unpeeled

2 bay leaves

1 bunch sage leaves

2 large Red Rooster potatoes, peeled

1 Bury black pudding

Unsalted butter

Salt and freshly ground white pepper

Pinch ground or freshly grated nutmeg

METHOD

Pre-heat the oven to 160ºC.

Warm the duck fat in a casserole, deep enough to cover the meat.

Add the pork, garlic, bay and sage leaves. Put a lid on and cook for 3 hours.

Next, cook the potatoes in salted water.

Drain well, mash until smooth, add butter, seasoning and nutmeg.

Keep warm or reheat in a microwave.

Turn up the oven to 180ºC.

Remove the pork from the fat, place in a roasting tray and cook until golden and crispy (about 15-20 minutes).

Remove the skin from the black pudding, slice and cook in the hot oven for 5 minutes on a tray. Keep warm.

Remove the pork from the oven, drain on a cooling wire but DO NOT REMOVE THE STRING.

Using a very sharp serrated knife, slice the pork into 5cm thick slices.

Remove the string with kitchen scissors.

TO SERVE

Place a good spoonful of mashed potato on a plate and place a slice of pork on top, with the cooked black pudding around the mash.

A separate gravy and apple sauce make good accompaniments.

BUYING IT, KEEPING IT

This dish is best if made 24-48 hours ahead. Get the butcher to tie the belly for you really neatly and tightly. Wrap the pork in tin foil, allow to cool, then refrigerate. Slice when cold and gently reheat in a microwave for a minute or two before putting it back in a hot oven to crisp up. The pork will keep for 2-3 days in the fridge. The duck fat can be reused many times.

BRAISED FEATHER BLADE OF BEEF

INGREDIENTS – SERVES 8

2kg feather blade of beef, all fat and sinew removed

Sunflower oil

50g unsalted butter

4 large onions, peeled and thinly sliced

Salt and freshly-ground pepper

1 litre beef stock

2 garlic cloves, finely chopped

2 bay leaves

1 dessertspoon sugar

1 x 500ml bottle of good ale or bitter

METHOD

Preheat the oven to 160ºC.

Take a deep enamel or ovenproof casserole big enough to take the full blade.

Heat the dish and add a splash of oil and butter.

Add the beef and colour all over until a dark brown.

Add the onion and season. Turn the heat down to 140ºC, put a lid on and cook for about 15 minutes until the onions have become golden.

Add the stock and bring to a simmer. Now take a wooden spoon and scrape the bottom of the pan to ensure all the flavour of the caramelised onions is blended into the stock.

Add the garlic, bay leaves and sugar and bring back to a simmer.

Taste for seasoning, add the beer and put the lid on. Cook for 3 and a half hours.

Remove from the oven and allow to rest, with the lid on, for 1 hour.

Remove the meat from the dish, remove the string and place on a chopping board and cut into thick 4-5cm slices.

Taste the sauce and adjust the seasoning if necessary.

TO SERVE

Mash and simple fresh vegetables are all you need.

FIRST FIND YOUR FEATHER

This dish is best made 24 hours ahead and reheated either in the microwave or in a little of the sauce.

Wine can be used instead of beer.

The 'feather' is a long piece of meat from inside the shoulder. Good butchers will know what you're talking about when you ask for this cut. DO NOT trust the supermarkets to come up with the goods. You'll be disappointed.

DUCK AND PORK RILLETTES

INGREDIENTS – SERVES 15

1 large duck, deboned, sinew removed and cut into 2cm pieces

4 large duck breasts, cut into 2cm cubes

500g pork fillet cut into 2cm cubes

1kg back fat, cut into 2cm cubes

1 large carrot

1 large onion

2 sticks celery

Parsley stalks, handful of sage leaves, 2 bay leaves (to make a bouquet garni)

6 large peeled garlic cloves

1 litre water

1 bottle dry white wine

2 dessertspoons Maldon sea salt

15g jar green peppercorns

METHOD

Place all the ingredients except the peppercorns into a heavy duty pan or enamel casserole.

Make the bouquet garni by tying up the parsley stalks, bay leaves and sage inside the celery with string.

Bring to a simmer and cook gently with a lid on for 3-4 hours until the meat is flaky and the fat soft.

Allow to cool slightly.

Remove the vegetables and bouquet garni.

When still slightly warm and using your fingers, flake the meat and mix in with the fat.

Add the peppercorns and mix all thoroughly.

Mould into jars or a cling film-lined terrine.

TO SERVE

With sourdough toast, pickles and chutneys.

STAR QUALITY

This recipe comes from Le Gavroche. There is a lot of prep but once made it will keep for weeks. It is great for picnics, barbeques and informal dinner parties.

Although this recipe makes one full terrine, it can be halved. The rillettes can be stored in jars or individual terrines.

LAKELAND
the home of creative kitchenware™

Serve with sourdough toast, pickles and chutneys on an attractive serving platter. (ref.42273)

SOUFFLÉ SUISSESSE

A Roux/Le Gavroche classic which I have slightly adapted. I have cooked this dish for over 30 years. It still blows people away.

INGREDIENTS – SERVES 4, YOU WILL NEED, FOIL PUDDING DISHES 8.5CM X 6CM

FOR THE PUDDING DISHES

50g softened unsalted butter

100g plain flour

FOR THE SOUFFLÉ BASE

65g plain flour

60g unsalted butter

1 pint milk

2 medium eggs, separated

Pinch of cayenne pepper

Pinch of ground nutmeg

Pinch of salt

FOR THE CREAMY SAUCE

1 pint double cream

250g grated Isle of Mull or mature Cheddar PLUS 300g of grated Cheddar to sprinkle on top of the soufflés

150g finely-grated Parmesan cheese

Salt and ground white pepper

Pinch of ground nutmeg

Pinch of cayenne

100g blanched spinach leaves

1 large or 2 small leeks, split lengthways, washed, drained, chopped and blanched

200g wild mushrooms (optional), chopped

(Continued overleaf...)

The Le Creuset 19cm rectangular dish is the perfect size for a double serving (ref.15144)

FOR THE PUDDING DISHES

Pre-chill the foil dishes in a fridge or freezer.

Pre-heat the oven to 225ºC .

Lightly brush the foil dishes with the butter. Sprinkle a dessertspoon of flour into each of the foil dishes so it coats the inside. Shake off any excess.

Keep the foil dishes in a cool place otherwise the butter will melt off the sides and the flour will become sticky.

FOR THE SOUFFLÉ BASE

Make a roux with the butter and flour, and allow to cool slightly.

Bring the milk to a boil with the cayenne, nutmeg and salt.

Whisk the roux until smooth, pour on the milk and whisk vigorously until thoroughly mixed.

Put the mixture back into the pan and place on the heat. Whisk continuously as it comes to the boil. Add the egg yolks and continue whisking until well blended.

Pour the soufflé "base" into a Pyrex bowl and cover with cling film.

FOR THE CREAMY SAUCE

Bring the cream to a gentle simmer with the cheese and seasonings.

To make and cook the soufflés gently warm the "base" in the Pyrex dish for 1 minute in a microwave.

Tip half of this mixture into a large mixing bowl and whisk until smooth.

Beat the egg whites with a pinch of salt until smooth and forming peaks.

Whisk 2 dessertspoons of the beaten whites into the base, then with a spatula or wooden spoon, fold in the remaining whites.

Spoon this mixture into the foil dishes but only fill them two-thirds full.

Place onto a baking tray and bake for 8 minutes.

Remove from the oven but allow to stand for 5 minutes before de-moulding.

In the meantime, place the spinach into individual serving dishes or one large dish.

Add the leeks to the cheese sauce and pour into the dish/dishes.

Carefully tip out the soufflé "bases" onto the sauce. Sprinkle with the extra grated cheese and re-bake for 12 minutes until golden brown and almost double in size.

NOTES

The thick "base" recipe makes too much for one serving of soufflés but it is difficult to make it effectively in a smaller quantity. You can use the leftover for a cheese sauce base – just let it down with extra heated milk and cream and add grated cheese. These soufflés are best baked in individual dishes, ovenproof gratin dishes being the best. However, it does make an impressive dish if baked altogether in a large dish and served at the table. Practice makes perfect, so have a couple of goes before trying to impress friends and family. Apart from the cheese and cream, it is a relatively inexpensive dish to produce and continues to wow after 45 years since it first appeared on the menu at Le Gavroche.

PAN-FRIED VENISON FILLET WITH BRAISED RED CABBAGE & SPICED APPLE RELISH

INGREDIENTS – SERVES 4

FOR THE VENISON
800g venison fillet

Freshly ground black pepper

Salt

Sunflower oil

75g butter

FOR THE SAUCE
50ml red wine

400ml good beef stock

1 teaspoon caster sugar

FOR THE BRAISED RED CABBAGE
2 onions – 1 sliced thinly, 1 left whole

3 cloves

1 dessertspoon duck fat or beef dripping

1kg red cabbage, sliced very finely

Salt and freshly ground pepper

250ml red wine

1 stick celery

1 carrot

1 bay leaf

2 dessertspoons dark brown sugar

500ml beef stock

FOR THE RELISH – MAKES 1.5KG
800g Bramley apples, peeled, cored and cut into 3cm chunks

200g sultanas

3 star anise

2 cinnamon sticks

3 cloves

200ml cider vinegar

250ml dry cider

Splash balsamic vinegar

75g dark brown sugar

75g golden sugar

Pinch salt

(Continued overleaf...)

A good lidded frying pan is helpful for this recipe (ref.14303) and a sharp slicing knife makes cutting the venison easy. (ref.13605)

METHOD

Allow the venison to come up to kitchen temperature (about 60 minutes).

Heat a lidded frying pan and add a splash of oil and the butter. When the butter is golden brown add the venison, season all over with salt and pepper and cook until it is coloured all over (about 10 minutes).

Drop the temperature and continue to cook slowly with the lid on for a further 5 minutes or 10 minutes if you want it well done.

Remove the meat from the pan and allow to rest for at least 10 minutes before serving.

FOR THE SAUCE

Drain off the fat from the pan, return to the heat, add the red wine and reduce by half.

Add the stock and reduce again by half.

Taste for seasoning and add the sugar.

Strain the sauce through a fine sieve

FOR THE BRAISED RED CABBAGE

Preheat the oven to 130ºC.

Stud the whole onion with the cloves.

Heat the fat in a thick-bottomed pan and sweat the red cabbage and sliced onion together.

Season lightly and continue to sweat with the lid on for about 10 minutes.

Add the wine and reduce by half.

Add the whole onion, celery, carrot, bay leaf and sugar and mix together well.

Add the stock, bring to a simmer and taste for seasoning.

Cover with greaseproof paper or aluminium foil, put a lid on and cook for 2.5-3 hours.

Allow to cool completely in the pan and store with the others components of the dish until required.

Remove the onion, celery, carrot and bay leaf before using.

FOR THE RELISH

Place all the ingredients into a large thick-bottomed pan, bring to a simmer and cook for about 30 minutes, stirring occasionally.

Mix well and allow to cool. Spoon into sterilised jars and seal.

TO SERVE

Gently warm the cabbage and relish in a microwave. Spoon the cabbage onto one large dish or individual plates. Carve the fillet and lay the slices on top of the cabbage. Pour the sauce over the meat. I like to serve this with fluffy roast potatoes or a nice buttery mash.

STEAK YOUR CLAIM

This recipe works equally well for 4 individual venison steaks instead of a whole fillet. The cabbage and relish is best made at least 1 day, if not a week, ahead.

Experiment by adding 125g diced smoked bacon or pancetta to the cabbage for a more pronounced flavour.

The cabbage stores nicely in the freezer.

SALMON ANTIBOISE

INGREDIENTS – SERVES 4

650-700g fillet of salmon

100ml sunflower oil

25g butter

FOR THE ANTIBOISE

250ml cooked tomato sauce

6 basil leaves, shredded

6 black olives, chopped

125ml olive oil

1 teaspoon garlic, crushed

4 mint leaves, shredded

Salt and freshly ground black pepper

Balsamic vinegar to serve

METHOD

Heat the oil and butter in a non-stick pan.

Lightly season the salmon. Place in the pan and colour on both sides.

Cook for 8-10 minutes. Remove from the pan, place in a dish and keep warm.

METHOD

Mix all the antiboise ingredients together and keep at room temperature.

TO SERVE

Spoon the sauce over the fish and dribble a few drops of balsamic vinegar over the sauce.

It's also good with pasta, grilled vegetables and chicken. The sauce will keep in the fridge for about 5 days.

LAKELAND
the home of creative kitchenware™

A good, solid sauté pan is an investment.
The Lakeland Tri-ply 24cm sauté pan is ideal. (ref.13190)

SALMON EN PAPILLOTE

INGREDIENTS – SERVES 4

4 x 150g salmon fillets

2 large carrots, peeled

1 small leek, split and washed

1 egg-sized piece ginger root, peeled

Teriyaki marinade

White wine

Sunflower or sesame oil

4 star anise

Ketsup Manis

Ground black pepper

4 sheets aluminium foil (30cm x 200cm each)

METHOD

Cut the carrot, leek and ginger into thin julienne strips.

Gently heat a 30cm non-stick frying pan with a teaspoon of oil.

Mix the vegetables and ginger together and sweat in the pan until soft. (Approximately 2-3 minutes.)

Remove from the pan and allow to cool.

Pre-heat the oven to 180°C.

Put a dessertspoon of the cooled vegetables on a sheet of the foil.

Place the salmon fillet on top and put another dessertspoon of vegetables on top of the salmon. Repeat with the three remaining salmon fillets.

Fold the foil around each salmon fillet to form a parcel but do not close.

Sprinkle each fish with a good splash of Teriyaki marinade, wine and Ketsup Manis.

Add a star anise to each parcel and finish with a twist of pepper.

Fold the foil over and seal the parcel.

Place on a baking tray and bake for 10 minutes.

TO SERVE

Put a parcel in front of each guest and allow them to open to release the lovely aromas.

MAKING SALMON SIMPLE...

This is a quick and easy way for cooking salmon. The parcels can be made a few hours ahead and kept chilled, but allow them to come to room temperature before cooking.

Kesup Manis is a thick, sweet Indonesian soy sauce. Star anise is available in most supermarkets and ethnic shops.

LAKELAND
the home of creative kitchenware™

A Lakeland Julienne Peeler will make light work of the vegetables. (ref.15806)

SAUSAGE, MASH & ONION GRAVY

INGREDIENTS – SERVES 4

SAUSAGE & MASH

2 large Red Rooster potatoes
12 thin-link Cumberland sausages
100-150g unsalted butter
Pinch of ground or grated nutmeg
Salt and freshly ground black pepper
Sunflower oil

FOR THE ONION GRAVY

4 large white onions, peeled and thinly sliced
500ml dry white wine
1 litre good beef stock in vac-pac pouches from a good supermarket (eg True Foods)
Salt and freshly ground black pepper
50g unsalted butter
2 dessertspoons sugar

METHOD

Peel, wash and cut up the potatoes.
Cook in lightly salted boiling water for about 20 minutes.
Brush the sausages with oil and either grill or pan fry them until golden all over.
Drain the potatoes, mash well with lots of butter and nutmeg.

FOR THE ONION GRAVY

In a thick-bottomed sauce pan melt the butter, add the onions and sweat without any colour, approximately 25 minutes.
Add the sugar and the white wine and cook until reduced to three quarters of original.
Add the stock, bring to a simmer and cook slowly until reduced by half.
Taste for seasoning.

TO SERVE

Place the mash in the middle of the plate and put the sausages in or on the mash.
Pour over the gravy.

STANDBY SOLUTIONS

The gravy can be made days ahead and stored in the fridge in jars or sealed containers.
Red wine or beer could be used instead of white wine.
The sugar is an important addition as it balances the acidity of the sauce and brings out the flavour of the onions.

LAKELAND
the home of creative kitchenware™

The gravy can be made days ahead and stored in the fridge then served from a gravy boat to prevent drips. (ref.12006)

SEAFOOD & SPINACH MACARONI

INGREDIENTS – SERVES 4

1 packet Ziti Napolitana macaroni

Olive oil

300g salmon fillet

Salt and freshly ground black pepper

500ml cooked tomato sauce

24 mussels, cooked

24 large prawns, peeled and cooked (approximately 250g)

1 packet fresh basil, shredded

1 packet spinach

1 teaspoon chilli, chopped

150g Parmesan cheese, grated

METHOD

Preheat the oven to 170°C.

Cook the pasta in a large pan of heavily salted water with a good splash of oil.

Drain in a colander, rinse under running cold water until cool, then drain and sprinkle on a little oil to stop it from sticking together.

Blanch the spinach in boiling water, then refresh in iced water and drain thoroughly.

Heat a large non-stick frying pan, add the salmon, season lightly and cook for 8 minutes.

When it is cool enough to handle, flake the fish.

In a large saucepan, heat the tomato sauce thoroughly then add the fish, mussels, prawns, spinach, basil and chilli.

Arrange the pasta in lengths in an oven-proof dish. Pour over the sauce, sprinkle with the Parmesan and bake for 25 minutes.

QUICK FIXES

Split the pasta in half to make it easier to use. A top quality ready-made tomato sauce can be used as can a ready-cooked seafood mix from the supermarket. Extra chilli can be added and either hot-smoked salmon or smoked salmon are good alternatives.

Use the large finger-sized chillis as these are not so hot.

Store your pasta in an airtight jar, like the 2 litre glass jar from the Delicious range. (ref.15670)

SLOW COOKED LAMB SHOULDER WITH PETITS POIS À LA FRANÇAISE

INGREDIENTS – SERVES 4

EQUIPMENT
You will need a thick roasting dish, perferably enamel

FOR THE LAMB
1 x 2kg boned and rolled shoulder of lamb
4 large onions, peeled and thinly sliced
6 cloves garlic peeled and chopped
350ml dry white wine
350ml meat stock
6 sprigs of fresh thyme
Splash sunflower oil
Salt and ground white pepper

FOR THE PETITS POIS
50g unsalted butter, diced
1 medium leek, pale green and white part only, cut into fine strips
200g frozen button onions
4 slices smoked pancetta or smoked streaky bacon cut into thin strips
340g frozen petit pois peas
half teaspoon caster sugar
2 Little Gem lettuce, finely shredded
Sea salt and freshly ground black pepper
12 large mint leaves, finely shredded
100ml white wine
100ml vegetable stock

METHOD

Pre heat the oven to 200°C.

Lightly season the lamb with salt and pepper and rub all over with a little oil.

Put the lamb into the roasting dish and cook for 25 minutes until golden.

Remove from the oven and turn the oven down to 140°C.

Add the onions, garlic and thyme to the dish and mix well.

Cover the dish with tinfoil and cook for 1 hour.

Take the dish from the oven and remove the foil. Give the onion mixture a good stir.

Add the wine, place on a low heat on top of the stove and bring to a simmer.

Add half the stock and bring back to a simmer.

Cover the dish, return it to the oven and cook for a further 1 hour.

Remove from the oven, add the remaining stock and return to the oven for a further 30 minutes. The onions should be golden and the sauce syrupy.

FOR THE PETITS POIS

In a thick-bottomed pan melt the butter and sweat the leek, button onions and pancetta without colour for 5 minutes.

Add the peas, lettuce and sugar, stir well and season with a little salt and pepper.

Cook for 2 minutes then add the mint, wine and stock and bring to a simmer.

Cover and cook over a very low heat for 15 minutes, stirring occasionally.

Taste for additional seasoning.

TO SERVE

Remove the meat from the dish and remove the string. Place on a large serving plate and spoon over the sauce. Serve with a spoon and a fork as the meat will fall off the bone. Spoon the peas onto the plate.

WORTH A MINT

The lamb can be sprinkled with some freshly-picked thyme leaves or shredded mint. Alternatively, try my own personal favourite by making a minted grain mustard mash to go with it. Additional mint can be added according to preference. Try adding baby cooked carrots to the peas.

STUFFED BREAST OF CHICKEN WITH A TARRAGON FARCE, WILD MUSHROOMS & PILAF RICE

INGREDIENTS – SERVES 4

FOR THE FARCE (STUFFING)

1 x 200g chicken breast, skinned and sinew removed, cut into 1cm diced pieces and kept chilled

1 egg white

300ml double cream

1 soupspoon tarragon, chopped

Pinch ground or freshly-grated nutmeg

Pinch salt and ground white pepper

FOR THE CHICKEN

4 x 200g-250g chicken breasts, skin on

8 slices Parma ham

500g fresh mixed wild mushrooms, trimmed, washed, drained and dried

Sunflower oil

100ml water or stock

METHOD

FOR THE FARCE (STUFFING)

Using a food processor, blend the chicken breast with the egg white until smooth.

Using a rubber spatula, clean the sides of the bowl to ensure all the meat is mixed up.

Slowly add half of the cream until the mixture is smooth and homogenous.

Place the mixture into a clean bowl and slowly add the remaining cream, tarragon, nutmeg and seasoning by hand.

Keep this mixture chilled.

FOR THE CHICKEN

Preheat the oven to 180ºC.

Slice each chicken breast so that the meat opens out flat but remains in one piece.

Fill with about 1 tablespoon of the farce mixture and carefully fold over the breast.

Wrap each breast with the ham then roll in aluminium and twist both ends to a tight 'sausage'. If the aluminium tears, start again. You will need a piece of foil 20cm x 30cm.

Place the 'sausages' on a baking tray and cook for 25 minutes.

Remove from the oven and allow to rest in the foil for at least 10 minutes before serving.

Drain off the juices from the cooked breast into a non-stick frying pan and heat gently.

Pour in a splash of oil, add the mushrooms and sauté gently for 3-4 minutes.

Season lightly then add the water or stock and cook for a further 2-3 minutes. Keep warm.

TO SERVE

Remove the foil from the chicken breast and slice into four or five slices. Serve on a bed of pilaf rice and spoon the mushrooms on top. Oyster or button mushrooms can be substituted for the wild mushrooms.

PORK TERRINE

INGREDIENTS – SERVES 15

FOR THE TERRINE

900g diced pork shoulder

350g diced pork liver

200g diced pork fat

1 teaspoon chopped garlic

3 dessertspoons parsley, chopped

Salt and freshly ground pepper

100ml dry white wine

3 dessertspoons onion, finely chopped

Pinch grated nutmeg

AFTER

3 medium eggs

8 slices Parma or Serrano ham

METHOD

Mix all of the terrine ingredients together and allow to marinate for 24 hours.

Preheat the oven to 160ºC.

Mince the mixture twice through the coarse plate of a mincer.

Add the eggs and mix well until well combined.

Line the terrine mould with overlapping ham slices. Make sure that they overhang the mould so that they can be wrapped over the top of the mixture.

Fill with the terrine mixture and cover the top with the overlapping ham.

Put a lid on the terrine and bake in a bain-marie for 1 hour and 25 minutes.

Remove from the oven and allow the terrine to cool before putting it in the fridge.

JUST ADD WATER

This is best made 48 hours before serving.

A bain-marie in this case is a deep roasting tray half filled with water. Put the tray in the oven first, then add hot water and gently put in the terrine. When the terrine has cooked, remove from the tray with an oven cloth or gloves first before removing the tray itself. It's quicker, easier and safer.

PICKLED ONIONS

INGREDIENTS – MAKES 3 X 500ML JARS

750g small pickling onions, peeled

500ml water

75g sea salt

500ml white wine vinegar

175g brown sugar

Pinch brown mace

15g fresh ginger root, sliced

10 white peppercorns

METHOD

Put the water and salt into a pan and bring to the boil.

Put the onions into a large bowl and pour the salted water over the onions.

Allow to stand for 1 hour then drain, then peel.

Combine the remaining ingredients in a saucepan, bring to the boil and simmer for 3 minutes.

Add the onions and simmer for a further 5 minutes.

Pack in sterilised jars, seal and cool.

Keep for 1 week before serving.

KNOW YOUR ONIONS

Steeping the onions makes peeling a lot easier. Try to find kilo bags of frozen peeled silverskin onions from a reputable wholesaler or deli which will save an incredible amount of time – and your sanity! Or get friendly with your local restaurant and ask them to source the frozen version for you.

the home of creative kitchenware™

Lakeland Clip Top Kilner Preserving Jars (ref. 16229)
are ideal for storing these.

RED TOMATO CHILLI CHUTNEY

INGREDIENTS – MAKES 2.25KG

1.5kg red tomatoes, peeled and roughly chopped

1kg cooking apples, peeled and chopped

1 red chilli, split lengthways, deseeded and finely chopped

1 green chilli, split lengthways, deseeded and finely chopped

225g onions, chopped

25g pickling spice

25g dry mustard

25g salt

300ml cider vinegar

225g sultanas

350g light brown sugar

METHOD

Place the tomatoes, apples, onion and chilli in a large pan.

Wrap the pickling spice in a muslin bag, add to the mixture and begin to simmer gently, pouring in a little water if it begins to stick.

Blend the mustard and salt with a little vinegar and stir into the mixture.

When the ingredients have softened, add the sultanas, sugar and remaining vinegar.

Continue to simmer, stirring all the time, until the chutney is thick and smooth.

Pour the mixture into sterilised jars and seal while hot. Store for 2 months before opening.

VINAIGRETTE

INGREDIENTS

25ml white wine vinegar

50g tarragon and herb mustard

250ml sunflower oil or mix half and half with olive oil

Pinch of ground white pepper

Salt

METHOD

Whisk together the vinegar, mustard, salt and pepper then slowly whisk in the oil.

A QUESTION OF BALANCE

Always use at kitchen temperature. This makes a powerful dressing so 40g of mustard is probably enough for most palates. It will keep for 1 month. Don't use all olive oil as it too strong a flavour. You can enhance the flavour with a little crushed garlic or add a drop or two of either walnut or truffle oil to make it really special

CUCUMBER PICKLE

INGREDIENTS – MAKES 300ML

4 medium cucumbers

1.5 teaspoon salt

150ml groundnut or sunflower oil

1 red chilli

1 teaspoon garlic puree

2 tablespoon soy sauce

25g caster sugar

2 tablespoon white wine vinegar

1 bunch spring onions

METHOD

Peel and de-seed the cucumbers then grate them.

Put into a sieve with a bowl underneath to catch the juices.

Sprinkle with salt and leave for 3 hours.

In a thick-bottomed pan place all the other ingredients except the spring onions.

Bring the pan to a simmer, add the cucumber, stir and cook for 2 minutes.

Remove the pan from the heat and allow to cool.

Finely chop the spring onions and add to the cucumbers when completely cold.

Taste for seasoning.

Pour the mixture into sterilised jars and seal while hot.

PEAR AND DAMSON CHUTNEY

INGREDIENTS – MAKES ABOUT 1.5KG

750g pears, peeled, cored and roughly chopped

Half tablespoon salt

250g damsons

125g onions, minced

125g sultanas

1 tablespoon orange rind, coarsely grated

Juice of 2 oranges

300g sugar

Half teaspoon cinnamon

1 teaspoon ground or freshly-grated nutmeg

1 teaspoon cayenne pepper

50g root ginger, minced

300g white wine vinegar

METHOD

Put all the ingredients except for the pears in a pan and simmer on a gentle heat until a syrupy consistency is reached.

Add the pears and cook until soft.

Pour the mixture into sterilised jars and seal while hot.

TOMATO SAUCE

INGREDIENTS – MAKES APPROXIMATELY 1 LITRE

2 x 400g tins chopped tomatoes

2 dessertspoons tomato purée

200g onions, roughly chopped

2 sticks celery, roughly chopped

2 teaspoons chopped garlic

150ml olive oil

50g sugar

Pinch cayenne

1 teaspoon dried oregano

1 teaspoon dried Herbes de Provence

Juice of 1 lemon

Salt and freshly ground pepper

METHOD

Place the tomatoes and tomato purée into a food blender or use a stick blender and whizz to a pulp.
Pour into a container.
Put the onions, celery and garlic into the blender or use a stick blender and blitz until smooth.
In a thick-bottomed pan, heat the olive oil, add the onion mix and sweat for 5 minutes.
Pour in the tomatoes, add the sugar, cayenne, dried herbs, lemon juice, salt and pepper and cook on a gentle heat for 45 minutes.

PILAF RICE

INGREDIENTS – SERVES 4

60g unsalted butter

60g onion, peeled and finely chopped

200g long grain rice

400ml boiling water

1 bay leaf

Salt and freshly ground pepper

METHOD

Preheat the oven to 200°C.

Melt the butter in a flameproof casserole, add the onion and sweat gently for 1 minute.

Add the rice, increase the heat very slightly and cook for about 2 minutes, stirring with a wooden spoon until the rice becomes translucent.

Pour on the boiling water, add the bay leaf and season sparingly with salt.

Cover and cook in the oven for 18 minutes.

Remove from the oven and leave the rice to rest, still covered, in a warm place for 8-10 minutes.

Discard the bay leaf, fork through the rice, season to taste and serve.

FLAVOUR TIP

Vegetable stock or vegetable stock cubes can be used instead of water.

SPICED PICKLED DAMSONS

INGREDIENTS – MAKES 4 X 500ML JARS

1kg damsons

450g brown sugar

300ml red wine

200ml red wine vinegar

2 cinnamon sticks

8 cloves

1 teaspoon coriander seeds

1 teaspoon allspice berries

5cm fresh root ginger, peeled and sliced

METHOD

Prick each damson and place in a pan on top of the stove.

In a saucepan, heat together the sugar, vinegar and red wine and dissolve.

Pour this syrup over the damsons, simmer for 5 minutes then remove the fruit from the pan.

Add the remaining ingredients to the syrup and simmer together for a further 10 minutes.

Sieve the syrup, place back on the heat and simmer again, reducing the quantity by half.

Put the damsons into sterilised jars and pour the syrup over them.

Wrap the jars in a cloth, place in a pan of water and bring to the boil for 10 minutes.

Leave to cool and keep in a dark place for 1 month before using.

RASPBERRY SAUCE

INGREDIENTS – MAKES APPROXIMATELY 500ML

340g frozen raspberries

175g caster sugar

150ml water

juice of a lemon

METHOD

Put the raspberries, lemon juice, caster sugar and water in a saucepan and bring to the boil.
Cook for 10 minutes, blend, sieve and allow to cool.

HOT APRICOT SAUCE

INGREDIENTS – MAKES APPROXIMATELY 500ML

300g very ripe apricots

75g caster sugar

200ml water

1 tablespoon mint leaves, finely snipped

METHOD

Halve the apricots and remove the stones.
Put the apricots, sugar and water into a saucepan and cook gently for about 10 minutes until tender.
Transfer to a blender and puree for 1 minute, then pass through a conical sieve.
Add the shredded mint.

TO SERVE

Hot, to retain all its aroma!

CHOCOLATE SAUCE

INGREDIENTS – MAKES APPROXIMATELY 500ML

250g bitter chocolate, chopped

300ml single cream

METHOD

Heat the cream in a saucepan until just beginning to bubble.
Add the chocolate and stir with a whisk.
Reduce the heat and cook the sauce until smooth.

CARAMELISED STRAWBERRY PASTRY WITH WHIPPED CREAM

INGREDIENTS – SERVES 4

1 punnet strawberries, de-stalked and sliced

1 tub of good quality vanilla bean ice cream

1 packet Jus-Rol puff pastry, pre-rolled

Plain flour

Icing sugar to dust

250ml raspberry sauce (See recipe)

METHOD

Preheat the oven to 230°C.

On a very lightly floured surface, cut the pastry into 4 10x8cm rectangles (use a paper template).

Dust the pastry with icing sugar and bake for 10-15 minutes until golden and glazed.

Allow to cool.

TO SERVE

Slice the pastries in half. Place one half on a plate and arrange the strawberries around and over the pastry. Carefully place a scoop of ice cream on top of the berries and pour over some raspberry sauce. Place the second half on top and dust with icing sugar.

THE BERRY THOUGHT

Any raspberry sauce left over can be used on other desserts and it also freezes well.

If you wish, the pastry can be cut into alternative shapes.

A combination of red fruits in season works well, so use a combination of blueberries, raspberries, strawberries and blackberries in the autumn.

Garnish with tiny mint leaves if you want.

Presentation is important. We've presented this dessert in Lakelands 'Delicious Mint' Bowls (ref. 15676)

APPLE AND CINNAMON FEUILLETÉ

INGREDIENTS – SERVES 4

8 sheets of filo pastry

6 Golden Delicious apples

155g unsalted butter

Raw cane light brown soft sugar

Pinch of cinnamon

Cognac or Calvados

Icing sugar for dusting

METHOD

Preheat the oven to 180°C.

Peel, quarter and core the apples then cut each quarter in two.

In a non-stick frying pan add 75g of butter and heat until golden.

Add the apples and cook until golden brown.

Add 1 dessertspoon of sugar, the cinnamon and a splash of Cognac or Calvados.

Allow the fruit to cool.

Melt the remaining butter in a saucepan.

Spread out the filo pastry, allowing 2 sheets per person and brush lightly with the butter.

Fill the middle of each with an equal amount of apple and fold and twist the pastry.

Brush with melted butter, put on a baking tray and bake for about 20 minutes until golden brown.

Lightly dust with icing sugar.

TO SERVE

Great served with mascarpone flavoured with Cognac or Calvados and a dessertspoon of icing sugar.

BANANA CAKE WITH SULTANAS & CHERRIES

INGREDIENTS – MAKES 1 X 2LB LOAF

2 medium bananas, peeled

70g sultanas, soaked in a pot of hot tea

70g glace cherries

90g unsalted butter, softened

90g Demerara sugar

2 medium eggs at room temperature, beaten

180g self-raising flour, sifted

2 teaspoon lemon juice

2 tablespoon olive oil

FOR THE GLAZE

100g clear honey, warmed

METHOD

Soak the sultanas in tea overnight. Drain.

Preheat the oven to 175°C.

Grease and line a loaf tin with baking paper.

In a large bowl, mash the bananas with a fork.

Cream together the butter and sugar, then mix the bananas in thoroughly.

Stir in half the egg and half of the flour and mix thoroughly.

Add the remaining flour and egg, lemon juice and olive oil, and mix to make a thick batter.

Fold in the cherries and sultanas.

Pour into the prepared tin and bake for 50 minutes.

Check the cake is ready by inserting a skewer, which should come out clean. If it needs longer to cook, reduce the temperature to 165°C and check again every 5 minutes.

FOR THE GLAZE

Remove cake from the oven and while still warm, stud the top with a skewer and brush with honey.

Lakeland My Kitchen 2LB Loaf Tin (ref.13646) and
Loaf Tin Liners (ref.5553) ensure non-stick results every time.

CARROT CAKE

INGREDIENTS

FOR THE CAKE

175g plain flour

¾ teaspoon baking powder

¾ teaspoon bicarbonate of soda

1 teaspoon ground cinnamon

¼ teaspoon ground cloves

¼ teaspoon ground nutmeg

¼ teaspoon ground ginger

3 medium eggs

275ml vegetable or sunflower oil

275g dark brown soft sugar

125g grated carrots

50g sultanas soaked in hot tea and allowed to cool

50g chopped walnuts

FOR THE TOPPING

95g softened unsalted butter

200g full-fat soft cheese

105g sifted icing sugar

Finely grated zest of 1 orange

METHOD

FOR THE CAKE

Pre-heat the oven to 170ºC.

Grease and line a 23cm cake tin.

Mix the sugar, oil and eggs together until well combined.

Add the flour, baking powder, bicarbonate of soda and spices.

Add the carrots, walnuts and soaked sultanas.

Put the batter into the tin and bake for about 45 minutes, until a skewer comes out clean.

Allow to cool for at least an hour.

FOR THE TOPPING

Beat the butter, cheese and icing sugar together to a thick cream then add the orange zest and mix in well. Spread the finished mixture evenly across the top of the cake.

CHOCOLATE FONDANT

INGREDIENTS – SERVES 5

125g 70% dark chocolate

125g unsalted butter

3 large eggs

150g caster sugar

35g soft plain flour, sieved

Unsalted butter and cocoa powder for dusting the moulds

METHOD

Preheat the oven to 190°C.

Melt the chocolate and butter slowly over a low heat in a pan.

Whisk in the eggs and sugar together until well combined, then add the flour.

Stir both mixtures together and pour into the buttered and dusted foil dishes.

Place the foil dishes on a baking sheet and bake for approximately 10-12 minutes.

The centre of the fondant should still be liquid once cooked.

TO SERVE

Demould on to one large or 4 individual plates and serve with a good quality vanilla ice cream, double cream or crème frâiche and raspberry sauce.

THE PERFECT FOIL

You can make up the mix in advance and it will last a few days.

You will need foil pudding dishes 8.5cm deep and 6cm deep.

LAKELAND
the home of creative kitchenware™

Individual servings fit perfectly in the Delicious Dip Bowls
(ref.15679)

CHOCOLATE NEMESIS

INGREDIENTS - MAKES 8

170g dark chocolate

110g diced unsalted butter

60ml water

140g caster sugar

3 medium eggs

METHOD

Pre-heat the oven to 180°C.

Melt the chocolate with the butter, water and 50g of the sugar.

Allow to cool slightly.

Whisk the eggs with the remaining sugar in a mixer for about 10 minutes.

Fold the chocolate mixture into the egg mixture very quickly.

Place a tray in the oven and half fill with warm water. (This is known as a bain-marie)

Pour into 10cm x 2cm deep moulds and place in the bain-marie in the oven.

Bake for about 50-60 minutes. The top should be crusty with a soft centre.

TO SERVE

Serve with a generous scoop of chocolate ice cream.

CHOCOLATE ROULADE

INGREDIENTS

3 medium eggs, separated

175g icing sugar

50g cocoa powder

15g cornflour

Pinch salt

FOR THE FILLING

300ml double cream

75g caster sugar

2 punnets raspberries

1 punnet strawberries

1 pot top quality raspberry jam

FOR THE DECORATION

Icing sugar

Fresh raspberry sauce

METHOD

Preheat the oven to 180°C.

Line a 38cm x 26cm Lakeland Multi-purpose Oven Tray with Lakeland Magic Non-stick Liner.

In a large mixing bowl, beat the egg yolks with 80g of the icing sugar for about 5 minutes.

In another bowl, lightly beat the eggs whites with the salt, add the remaining icing sugar and beat until the soft peak stage, about 30 seconds to 1 minute longer.

Sift together the cocoa powder and cornflour.

Using a spoonula, start to fold the cocoa mix into the egg yolk mix, add one tablespoon of egg white at a time until all the cocoa and eggs whites are incorporated.

Spread the mixture over the baking tray using a spoonula or an angled spatula and bake for about 8 minutes until the top of the sponge feels springy when pressed with the fingertips.

Remove the sponge base from the oven and allow to cool for about 4-5 minutes.

Flip the sponge base on to a sheet of greaseproof paper, peel off the magic non-stick liner (you can wash and re-use it) and allow to cool for a further 3-4 minutes.

FOR THE FILLING

Gently whisk the cream with the sugar until firm but do not overbeat.

Spread the jam over the sponge, spread the cream on top then dot with the fruit.

Using the paper, roll the roulade tightly but quickly. Use the ends to twist the paper like the ends of a Christmas cracker.

Put into the fridge and allow to rest for at least 1 hour before required.

TO SERVE

Remove the roulade from the fridge and dust with icing sugar. Trim the ends and slice into 3cm thick slices and serve with a fresh raspberry sauce. Blackberries, wild strawberries and blueberries are good alternatives too.

CHOCOLATE STOUT CAKE

INGREDIENTS

FOR THE CAKE

250ml Guinness or Murphy's stout

250g unsalted butter

75g cocoa powder

400g caster sugar

140g sour cream

2 medium eggs

1.5 teaspoon vanilla extract

275g plain flour

2.5 teaspoon bicarbonate of soda

FOR THE TOPPING

225g soft cream cheese

110g icing sugar, sifted

90ml double cream

METHOD

FOR THE CAKE

Grease a deep loose-bottomed 23cm cake tin and line with baking parchment.

Pre-heat the oven to 170°C.

Pour the stout into a large saucepan, place on the stove over a gentle heat, then add the butter until melted.

Whisk in the cocoa and sugar.

Beat the sour cream and vanilla with the eggs and pour into the stout mixture.

Stir together the flour and bicarbonate of soda and finally whisk this into the mixture.

Pour the mixture into the lined tin and bake for 50 minutes. Check that a skewer comes out clean after inserting it in the middle of the cake.

If it needs longer, reduce the temperature to 160°C and check every 5-10 minutes.

Leave the cake in the tin to cool completely as it will still be quite moist.

FOR THE TOPPING

Beat the icing sugar and cream cheese until smooth then add sufficient cream to achieve a spreadable consistency.

the home of creative kitchenware™

Serving can be made easy by using an
Angled Spatula (ref. 11840)

COFFEE CAKE

INGREDIENTS

FOR THE CAKE

200g plain flour

225ml sunflower oil

225g dark soft brown sugar

3 medium eggs

3 tablespoons strong coffee

1 teaspoon baking powder

FOR THE TOPPING/FILLING

125g unsalted butter

160g icing sugar

250g cream cheese

2 tablespoons strong coffee

METHOD

Pre-heat the oven to 170ºC.

Grease and line a 23cm cake tin.

Mix the sugar, oil and eggs together until well combined.

Add the coffee and mix well.

Add the flour and baking powder.

Put the batter into the tin and bake for about 40 minutes, until a skewer comes out clean.

Cool on a wire rack then split in two.

For the topping, beat the butter, cheese and icing sugar together to a thick cream then add the coffee and mix in well.

HONEY, WHISKEY & DRAMBUIE CRÈME BRÛLÉE

INGREDIENTS – MAKES 10

287ml double cream

57g warmed honey

4 large egg yolks

62g caster sugar

17ml whisky

42ml Drambuie

EQUIPMENT

10 round ovenproof moulds, 10.5cm x 2cm deep

1 propane gas blow torch

METHOD

Pre-heat the oven to 180ºC.

Whisk together the egg yolks, 25g sugar, honey, whisky and Drambuie.

Bring the cream to the boil and whisk thoroughly into the egg mixture.

Strain through a fine sieve.

Place the moulds into a shallow tray and pour in the mixture.

Place the tray in the oven and half fill with warm water. (This is known as a bain-marie.)

Cook for approximately 35 minutes. It should be set but not wobbly.

Remove the brûlées from the oven and allow to cool for at least 1 hour before glazing.

Sprinkle with the remaining sugar and glaze using the blow torch.

CRACKING STUFF

Warm the honey in the jar in a microwave (without the lid!) for a few seconds.

Cook the brûlées in a non-fan assisted oven otherwise the surface will crack.

They can be made a day ahead and gently microwaved for a few seconds before glazing.

When glazing, hold the moulds in a cloth in case hot caramel runs down the sides.

LAKELAND
the home of creative kitchenware™

In the hands of a serious cook, the Lakeland blowtorch becomes a magic wand! (ref.16416)

TUILE WITH SEEDS

INGREDIENTS – MAKES ABOUT 24 'TILES'

200g caster sugar
50g sesame seeds
50g poppy seeds
100g unsalted butter, melted
100ml orange juice
100g plain flour

Zest of 1 orange
Sunflower oil

METHOD

Mix all the ingredients together except for the oil and rest for 24 hours.

Pre-heat the oven to 180°C.

Oil two 26cm x 38cm trays and line with Lakeland Magic non-stick liner.

Using a soup spoon, spoon out identically-sized mounds of the mixture, spacing them evenly.

Dip a fork into a glass of cold water and press down lightly on each mound with the back of the fork to make a sort of very thin pancake, about 7cm in diameter and of even thickness. Dip the fork into the water for each tuile.

Cook for about 5-6 minutes until the tuiles are a delicate golden colour.

Remove from the oven and allow to cool for 1 minute before sliding them off with a palette knife and placing carefully over rolling pins to create the tuile shape.

Leave for a minute to set.

The tuiles, literally meaning tiles, can be made 2-3 days ahead and stored in airtight containers. The Lakeland Magic non-stick liner can be re-used.

FLAPJACK

In our humble opinion this is one of the best flapjack recipes. It is essential to use jumbo oats – normal oats will result in a cardboard-like texture.

INGREDIENTS – MAKES 1 26CM X 38CM TRAY

375g unsalted butter
300g golden syrup
100g light brown soft sugar
2kg jumbo oats

METHOD

Preheat the oven to 170°C.
Line a baking tray with greaseproof paper.
In a heavy-bottomed pan, add the butter, syrup and sugar and bring to the boil.
Add the oats and mix thoroughly.
Pour into the tray and spread the mixture evenly.
Bake in the oven for 20–25 minutes or until golden.
Remove from the oven and allow to cool before tipping out, peeling off the paper and cutting into the desired size.

LAKELAND
the home of creative kitchenware™

It's essential when baking 'tray bakes' to have a heavy duty
Swiss Roll baking tin. (ref. 12289)

FLOURLESS CHOCOLATE CAKE

INGREDIENTS – TO MAKE 2 X 25CM CAKES

450g dark chocolate

225g unsalted butter and extra for buttering

320g caster sugar

10 medium eggs, separated

FOR THE GANACHE

350g dark chocolate

150g unsalted butter

425ml double cream

METHOD

Pre-heat the oven to 165ºC.

Thoroughly butter 2 x 25cm springform pans.

Melt the butter and chocolate together in a bowl over a pan of simmering water.

In a separate bowl, whisk together the eggs yolks and 125g of sugar until pale and creamy.

Add the chocolate mixture to the egg mixture and combine thoroughly.

Whisk the egg whites until these start to become firm.

Gradually whisk in the remaining sugar until the mixture forms stiff peaks.

Fold the egg whites into the chocolate mixture.

Divide between the two prepared pans and bake for about 1 hour and 15 minutes.

Remove from the oven and turn out onto a wire rack to cool.

The tops may crack while cooling, but this is normal.

FOR THE GANACHE

Break the chocolate into an electric mixer bowl using a beater.

Boil the cream and add to the chocolate and start to mix slowly then add the butter.

Allow to cool and thicken then use as a filling and topping.

HONEY MADELEINES

2 medium eggs

75g caster sugar

10g dark soft brown sugar

Pinch salt

90g plain flour

1 teaspoon baking powder

90g unsalted butter, melted and cooled
plus 30g extra for greasing

1 tablespoon clear honey

METHOD

Preheat the oven to 220°C.

Combine the eggs, both sugars and salt into a bowl and work lightly with a spatula until the mixture begins to turn light in colour.

Sift together the flour and baking powder and fold gently into the mixture without overworking it.

Pour in the butter and honey and mix thoroughly.

Cover the bowl with cling film and leave to rest in a cool place for about 30 minutes.

Brush the insides of a Lakeland My Kitchen Madeleine Pan with the extra butter.

Pipe the mixture into each mould (see photograph).

Bake in the oven for about 8-10 minutes. Don't overcook or they will lose their distinctive moist texture.

Remove carefully from the pan onto a cooling wire.

TO SERVE

Immediately! They are best enjoyed fresh. Great with a cup of tea or coffee.

HOT LEMON SOUFFLÉ WITH LEMON CURD

FOR THE CREAM BASE

1 pint milk

125g caster sugar

6 medium egg yolks

50g plain flour

Zest from 3 lemons and juice of 2

FOR THE EGG WHITE BASE

Unsalted butter, softened for greasing the moulds

150g caster sugar (you will need a little extra for dredging the moulds)

8 medium egg whites

FOR THE LEMON CURD

85g sugar

4 medium eggs

125g butter

Zest and juice of 3 small lemons

METHOD

Preheat the oven to 220ºC.

Bring the milk to the boil.

Whisk together the sugar, flour, egg yolks, lemon zest and juice.

Pour the milk over the mixture and combine then return all to the pan.

Whisk continuously until the mixture is brought back to the boil.

Boil for 30 seconds. Remove from the heat and pour into a bowl and keep warm.

Brush each mould with the softened butter and dredge with the extra caster sugar.

In another bowl, beat the egg whites with a pinch of sugar until well risen.

Gently add the egg whites to the pastry cream.

Fill the moulds, smooth the surface with a palette knife and push the mixture away from the edge with the point of a knife.

Bake for 10-12 minutes.

Serve with lemon curd.

FOR THE LEMON CURD

Mix all the ingredients in a bain-marie.

Cook at blood temperature for about 30 minutes, stirring continuously.

TIMESAVING TIP

The cream base can be made a day ahead and simply rewarmed in a microwave.

LEMON DRIZZLE CAKE

INGREDIENTS – MAKES 1 X 2LB LOAF

FOR THE CAKE

180g unsalted butter, softened, or margarine

180g caster sugar

3 large eggs

180g self-raising flour

Zest of 1 lemon

Juice of half a lemon

FOR THE DRIZZLE

Juice of half a lemon

150g caster sugar

Water

FOR THE TOPPING

100g unsalted butter, softened

100g icing sugar, sifted

Juice of 1 lemon

Zest of half lemon

METHOD

FOR THE CAKE

Preheat the oven to 170ºC. Grease and line the loaf tin with baking paper.

Beat the butter or margarine until creamy then add the sugar and beat until fluffy.

Beat in the eggs then fold in the flour.

Add the zest and juice.

Pour the batter into the prepared tin and bake for 45 minutes.

Remove the cake from the oven and allow to stand for about 30 minutes.

FOR THE DRIZZLE

Make the drizzle by boiling together the lemon juice and sugar with a splash of water until the sugar has dissolved.
Stud the top of the cake using a Lakeland re-usable cake tester and brush while the drizzle is still hot.

FOR THE TOPPING

Beat the butter and icing sugar together until creamy and add the juice and zest and beat well.

When the cake is completely cold, spread the top with the butter icing.

Decorate with lemon zest if desired.

KEEP IT TOGETHER

Adding the lemon juice and zest after the flour has been folded in reduces the chance of the mixture splitting.

the home of creative kitchenware™

Rather than testing cakes with the prod of a finger, ensure they're baked to perfection the professional way with the Lakeland re-usable cake tester. (ref.10711)

SCONES

INGREDIENTS

750g self-raising flour

125g unsalted butter

125g caster sugar

125g sultanas

300ml buttermilk or milk with a squeeze of lemon juice

2 medium egg yolks and a splash of milk for the glaze

METHOD

Sift the flour and rub in the butter. Add the sugar and sultanas and for best results leave to rest overnight.

Next day, pre-heat the oven to 180°C.

Add the soured milk to the mixture and knead lightly.

Tip out onto a floured surface and roll to a thickness of approximately 4cm.

Use a 7.5cm cutter to stamp out your scones. This recipe will make about 10 really big scones or up to 20 smaller ones.

If you use a smaller cutter to make more scones the cooking time should be amended.

Place on a non-stick baking sheet, brush with the beaten egg yolks and milk and cook for about 16 minutes.

Remove from the oven, allow to cool for at least half an hour before serving.

STRAWBERRY SHORTBREAD

INGREDIENTS – MAKES 24 BISCUITS

250g plain flour

200g unsalted butter softened

100g caster sugar

3 medium egg yolks

400g strawberries, cut in half lengthways

Raspberry sauce (see recipe)

Icing sugar for dusting

METHOD

In a bowl, beat the sugar with the butter until creamy.

Add the eggs yolks one at a time until thoroughly mixed in.

Rub in the flour by hand.

Divide the mixture into 2 parts. Roll each one into a sausage shape about 6cm in diameter.

Wrap each sausage in cling film and put in the fridge for at least 1 hour before use.

Pre-heat the oven to 200°C.

On a lightly floured marble slab or wooden surface, slice the pastry into approximately 1.25cm rounds. Roll out until about 8cm and cut with a fluted cutter.

Transfer immediately on to a baking sheet lined with Lakeland Magic Non-stick Liner, leaving enough space between each one to allow the pastry to spread whilst cooking.

Bake for about 5 minutes. Allow to cool slightly then transfer to a wire rack.

TO ASSEMBLE

Put a biscuit on each plate, arrange some strawberries on top and pour the raspberry sauce over them. Top with another biscuit and dust with icing sugar.

TO SERVE

The biscuits can be made 2 days ahead as long as they are kept in an airtight container. Double cream or vanilla ice cream make good accompaniments.

LAKELAND
the home of creative kitchenware™

Cookie-cutters will give your shortbread biscuits
a more professional finish (ref.15242)

TARTE TATIN

A classic French recipe, still one of my favourite desserts. The caramelising takes a bit of practice but once mastered, it's easy. Although Tarte Tatin moulds can be bought, a sauté pan is ideal.

INGREDIENTS – SERVES 4

EQUIPMENT NEEDED

24cm sauté pan

FOR THE TARTE TATIN

6 large Cox's apples, peeled,
cored and cut into halves

60g caster sugar

60g unsalted butter

Jus-Rol puff pastry, cut into 25cm circle

METHOD

Pre-heat the oven to 180°C.

Place the butter and sugar into the sauté pan and place the apples cut edge up.

Place the pan over a low heat and slowly caramelise the apples until golden brown.

Allow this to cool before placing the circle of pastry on top.

Put the pan in the oven for approximately 25-30 minutes.

Allow the tatin to stand for 10 minutes before turning out.

TEA BRACK

INGREDIENTS – MAKES 1 X 2LB LOAF

150g dark brown sugar

170ml hot tea

45ml dark rum

150g sultanas

1 large egg, beaten

150g soft plain flour

1 teaspoon baking powder

1 teaspoon mixed spiced

100ml warmed honey for glazing

METHOD

Dissolve the sugar in the tea, add the rum and sultanas and leave to soak overnight.

Pre-heat the oven to 160ºC.

Line a loaf tin with baking parchment, or use a disposable non-stick baking case.

Add the egg, flour, baking powder and mixed spice to the fruit mixture and mix well.

Pour into the prepared tin and bake for 1 hour or until a skewer comes out clean.

Remove from the oven and brush with the warmed honey.

THE REAL LEMON TART

INGREDIENTS – MAKES 2 TARTS

THE FILLING

12 Size 3 eggs

2 medium egg yolks, beaten

454g caster sugar

6 lemons, (the finely-grated zest and juice)

350ml double cream

FOR SWEET PASTRY

450g plain flour

150g icing sugar

225g unsalted butter at kitchen temperature

2 medium eggs

1 tablespoon milk

METHOD

FOR THE FILLING

Beat the eggs with the yolks and add the sugar, lemon juice and zest and then beat into the cream.

Allow to stand for 1 hour then strain through a fine sieve or chinois.

FOR SWEET PASTRY

Pre-heat the oven to 160°C.

Rub the butter and sugar together.

Add one egg, together with the flour and milk.

Bring all the ingredients together to a smooth paste and roll out into a 15cm round.

Wrap in cling film and chill for half an hour.

TO MAKE THE TART

Roll out the pastry and line a 20cm loose-based sandwich tin.

Line the base with a circle of greaseproof paper, fill with baking beans and bake for 20 minutes until golden and dry.

Remove the beans and allow the base to cool slightly. Remove the paper.

Separate the remaining egg, beat the yolk and brush the inside of the pastry base with it.

Return to the oven and bake for 5 minutes to seal it properly.

Pour in the mixture and cook for 75 minutes.

Allow to rest for 1 hour before serving.

LAKELAND
the home of creative kitchenware™

A loose-based sandwich tin makes removing the tart easier.
(ref.10986)

TUNISIAN STYLE ORANGE & ALMOND CAKE

INGREDIENTS

FOR THE CAKE

45g slightly stale breadcrumbs or gluten-free breadcrumbs

200g caster sugar

100g ground almonds

1.5 teaspoon baking powder or gluten-free baking powder

200ml sunflower or vegetable oil

4 medium eggs

Finely grated zest of 1 large orange

Finely grated zest of half a lemon

FOR THE SYRUP

85g sugar

2 cloves

1 cinnamon stick

Juice of 1 orange

Juice of half a lemon

METHOD

Mix the breadcrumbs with the sugar, almonds and baking powder.

Add the oil and eggs and beat well. Stir in the orange and lemon zest.

Pour the mixture into a greased 20cm cake tin.

Put into a cold oven and set the heat to 190ºC.

Bake for 40-45 minutes until a rich brown.

Whilst the cake cools, bring all the ingredients for the syrup gently to the boil in a pan, stirring until the sugar has dissolved.

Simmer for 3 minutes.

When the cake is cooked, cool in the tin for 5 minutes then turn out onto a plate.

Remove the cloves and cinnamon from the syrup, pierce holes in the cake with a skewer whilst still warm and pour the syrup over it.

Leave to cool, spooning the syrup over the cake every now and then until it is all soaked up.

LAKELAND
the home of creative kitchenware™

Presented on the Lakeland Oak Chopping Board (ref.15591)

THE CAFÉ

It is as much of a challenge running the First Floor Café as it is to work in some of the most exalted kitchens in the land.

Cooking outstanding basic food is a task in its own right. But doing it for up to 700 people on a busy day is another thing entirely. And that's what makes the place what it is.

The café is always busy and there's a wonderful buzz about the place. It attracts the complete spectrum of customers, from families on holiday with small children and pensioners making a day of it to business people coming in for a breakfast meeting and individuals just wanting a lunch break.

You'll find people reading a paper, checking their smart phones, working on their laptops, or just having a chat and a gossip.

On a typical day, customers start piling in from mid-morning. Many travel a fair distance to get here. They come for a look round Windermere, to do some shopping in Lakeland and to come to the First Floor Café for lunch. They see it as a treat and we're aware of that and we make it as special as we can for them.

When we first came here we listened to what Lakeland wanted because we're on the first floor of their flagship store and we had to reflect that. The consensus was that it needed to be bright, eclectic and modern. And I think that's how it is now.

For the look of the place we went for natural stone and wood, and gently shaded furnishings. The giant picture windows overlooking Windermere and the fells beyond add to what is a relaxing and contemporary feel.

FIRST
FLOOR

AT LAKELAND

Lakeland is a visitor destination in itself, so the majority of our customers can be seen heading up the stairs clutching shopping bags full of the latest must-haves for the kitchen. They come here for well prepared and well-cooked food, which rounds the day off nicely after a spot of retail therapy.

Be all things to all people – a lot of businesses fail when they do that – and we deliver efficiently (customers don't like waiting).

The café though is nothing without the people behind it and we're fortunate to have a really good team working here – in the kitchens, in the reception area and waiting on tables. They're cheerful and they meet everyone with a smile. Nothing should be too much trouble in a restaurant.

The menus change and may include dishes such as homemade soup and quiches, baked goat's cheese salads, grilled smoked kippers, Cumberland sausage baguettes, chargrilled breast of chicken with black pudding, seared fillet of fresh salmon and slow cooked lamb shank.

We use Farrer's tea and coffee, all of which is ethically and responsibly sourced. And we're quite proud of our cafetiere coffee, which is a blend of Columbian, Kenyan and Honduran beans, while we use a mix of South American beans roasted continental style in our bean-to-cup coffee machines.

Tea drinkers swear by our Farrer's Lakeland blend tea, but the choice extends to Earl Grey and a selection of herbal teas too. Our soft drinks include ginger beer and dandelion & burdock, names that will conjure up memories for many customers.

Our sweet things range from a plain shortbread to a chocolate cake filled and topped with a rich ganache. There's also Tunisian orange and almond cake, raspberry or mango sorbet, lemon drizzle cake, fruit tea loaf, chocolate chip cookies, syrup sponge and custard, and sticky toffee pudding and more.

I've always had a vision about what I wanted here… a vision of the food going out, a vision of how the kitchen works and a vision of the customers enjoying what we produce.

We're unique in what we're doing here and with what we're offering. And people appreciate that. You just have to look in the café and see how busy it is, and see how much people are enjoying themselves.

please pay
here →

please
pay here

LAKELAND

SHOP TALK – THE LAKELAND STORY

It's a place all cooks love, and to many it's as much a part of the Lake District as the Lakes themselves.

But few among the thousands who daily make for Lakeland's flagship head office and showroom in Windermere could possibly imagine how this, the company that is a byword for kitchenware right across the nation, started life.

It's the classic success story which began back in 1963.

Alan Rayner had just gone into business selling animal feed to local farmers, and poultry at Kendal market. He favoured packing meat in the new-fangled polythene bags, and quickly noticed how it sold better than other stallholders' produce. Farmers found it easier to store in their big chest freezers. Before long there was a huge demand for Alan's plastic bags and he realised he'd discovered a niche in the market.

Working from the garage of his home in Windermere, Alan and his wife Dorothy created a mail-order business – Lakeland Poultry Packers – supplying agricultural plastics and home-freezing bags. The couple's sons, Sam, Julian and Martin, earned pocket money helping to count the bags into packs of 100 ready for sale. This turned out to be valuable training for the boys, who took over the company when their father retired in 1974 and who are still at the helm today.

As the business grew, it relocated from the garage, changed its name to Lakeland Plastics, and moved away from agricultural products to "Everything for Home Freezing" and eventually "Everything for Home Cooking" too.

One of the original mail-order pioneers, the company started out with a six-page, black and white leaflet but, as the years went by, progressed to mailing full-colour catalogues. Lakeland creates about 18 catalogues every year and has an award-winning website too.

The creation of a permanent home next to Windermere station – where the company has its imposing head office, call centre and showpiece store – was followed by a change of name. Henceforth it would simply be known as Lakeland. Internet shopping, an iPad app and a customer advisory service by email as well as phone, have cemented the move into the 21st century.

Lakeland now employs some 2,000 staff, not just in its modern flagship store, but in its customer service centre and offices in Windermere, at its distribution centre in Kendal, and in its stores up and down the country.

That complex is also home to the First Floor café. It's an essential stopping-off point where visitors can relax after browsing the huge showroom, with its 206 types of baking tin and 89 different knives.

Despite its growth, diversity and the innovative approach it takes to the products it sells, Lakeland retains the values instilled by Alan Rayner, who believed above all in looking after the customer.

As Sam Rayner says: "We understand what our customers expect and want, which is to be innovative without being fashionable. They expect to find traditional things like foil and cake tins, but they also want something different and a little bit exciting. We won't sell £2.99 frying pans that won't last five minutes because our customers want products that are functional, practical and good value. And we enhance all that with exceptional service."

It's clear that Lakeland customers appreciate the personal touch. In the open plan call centre, staff are ready to deal with any inquiry, from"Will this cake tin be all right to use with this recipe?" to "Do you still sell mould cleaner?" or "Have you got a garlic press that doesn't need dismantling to clean it?" .

"Customers also ask us what the weather is like in Windermere or whether we can see the lake," says Sam. "But it's all part of the Lakeland service. We do our best to help people and we also try to make it a one-stop shop so if someone calls in, they talk to one person who can hopefully answer their queries without having to pass them on.

"We have great people here and in all our stores who make sure that the service and ambience that you find in Windermere is replicated throughout the company."

INSIDE LAKELAND

So you're just browsing, that's all. Or you're here just for that one item you need to whip up that recipe tonight.

Many visitors come with those aims firmly in mind – but thousands every day discover far more than they bargained for. Because this isn't just any store. This is Lakeland. So prepare to open up a whole new world of possibilities.

There are products you never knew existed, tools for a particular job you needed a helping hand with or things you simply would love to have in your home.

Windermere-based Lakeland has nearly 60 shops around the UK and in each one, staff never tire of hearing customers express astonishment at the unexpected gems awaiting them – the gadget or the implement you wonder how you ever got by without.

Shoppers might have a determined look on their faces when they arrive or they might just want to meander, but most will leave clutching the bright yellow handles of a distinctive blue Lakeland carrier bag containing an assortment of goodies. It's that kind of place.

A typical day at the flagship store in the heart of the Lakes will see grandparents visiting with their grandkids, parents with their children, and couples and individuals who have been recommended by relatives or friends.

It's not unusual to meet regular customers who have travelled long distances to make a day of it at the Windermere store. The message is clear. They trust the company and so it's well worth the journey.

With an awe-inspiring range of 4,000 products, all of them exhaustively tried and tested before receiving the Lakeland seal of approval, there's little any cook couldn't find.

These days, Lakeland still sells its legendary freezer bags and foil that's 30 per cent thicker than most others. But its food storage ideas have now extended into space-saving boxes and containers featuring the latest silicone seals or easy on-and-off lids, right through to clever vacuum systems that make food last so much longer.

please pay here

Seasons are reflected at each store by displays that mark the approach of spring, summer or Christmas. But there are some constant themes. Tap into a new kitchen, cooking or homeware trend and you'll want the right tools and equipment to go with it. You'll find it find it all here.

Home baking has always been popular with Lakeland devotees and the company has sold bun cases from day one. In recent years, cupcake making has become hugely popular and that's reflected in the range, which includes an array of fancy cake cases, mixers and cutters to icing tools for the most wonderful finishing touches.

Lakeland has always known its customers love preserving, and novices to experienced jam-makers alike can find everything they need, from jars of every size to covers and kits to ensure preserves are presented in the most attractive way.

Home bread-makers are catered for too, but you don't need to be an experienced baker to appreciate Lakeland's products.

Cooking is a part of daily life and the shelves boast serious pots, pans and cookware that would earn their keep in the busiest of professional kitchens, as well as basic ranges for those just starting out or filling a few gaps in their cupboards.

So far has Lakeland come that these days, it even develops its own products, including pots, pans and baking tins.

In the stores there are shelves stacked with gadgets that customers never knew they needed until they saw them at Lakeland – small, innovative tools to make preparing food easier. But there are also the "wish list" electricals such as sleek food processors, while the gleaming coffee makers and grinders reflect the quest of coffee lovers for that perfect cup.

Home solutions include products that help clean and protect, launder, store and organise. It's all about making the most of your home, taking care of what you've got and finding innovative solutions to everyday problems.

Space-saving and keep-things-tidy ideas have always been popular at Lakeland and the company has developed a whole range of products that utilise every inch of space.

As customers regularly say: "This place is full of really good ideas."

Listening to customers is what Lakeland is good at – and customer feedback is always considered at the start of any design. The search for new products is never-ending, and takes in suggestions from customers as well as from product inventors who have devised exciting new gadgets.

Every item in the range is put through its paces in the test area at Windermere which appropriately enough looks remarkably like a home kitchen. After all, that's the sort of place most items will end up. If a product doesn't come up to scratch – it won't find its way on to the shelves. It's as simple as that. Even products that have been around for a decade or two are regularly evaluated to make sure they still do the job effectively and efficiently.

THE COOK'S ESSENTIAL ARMOURY

There are gadgets and there are essentials in any kitchen. Here's a short-list of the basics every cook should have at their disposal.

KNIVES – good quality knives are essential. A chef's favourite will be a 10/12″ chopping knife because it's so versatile as it can be used for slicing, chopping and dicing.

CHOPPING BOARD – a beech board at least 20cm x 30cm in size, the bigger the better. Wood is scientifically proven to be more hygienic than plastic etc. and your knife doesn't slip working on a wooden board therefore it feels safer.

PANS – heavy-duty ware lasts so much longer and is essential when cooking on a regular basis.

STICK BLENDER – to make silky smooth sauces and soups easily and speedily.

KITCHEN SCALES – you cannot work without accurate scales to give you consistent recipes, especially for baking and pastry making.

DIGITAL THERMOMETER PROBE – it tells you when meat is cooked through, essential for poultry and pork so it is safe to eat.

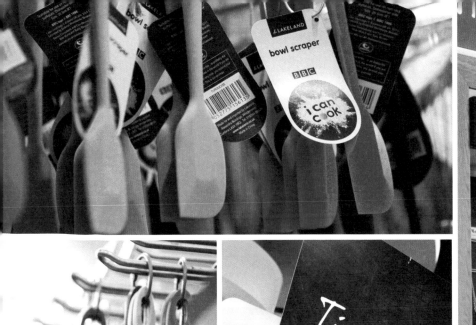

bowl scraper

BBC
i can
cook

chef's selection

Time Savers

chopping & grating

Joseph
Joseph

My
Kitchen

My Kitchen
Meat Mincer

£99.99

RECIPE INDEX